Meet 'The Other Petro[sian]'

When he had to defend, the 6th World Champion metamorphosed into a fearless adventurer who searched for counterplay at the cost of almost anything. Petrosian would make exchange sacs, spoil his pawn structure, march his King into danger if only it led to active play and dynamic opportunities.

Former Russian Champion Alexey Bezgodov introduces 'The Other Petrosian', and shows his extraordinary defensive skills.

In many training programs, a serious analysis of the art of defence is lacking. That explains why most club players (and lots of masters, as well) are much better at attacking than at coping with adversity and difficult positions.

Defend Like Petrosian will improve the standard of your defensive play by teaching how to find creative solutions when under attack. It will help you save lots of points!

paperback | 272 pages | €24.95 | available at your local (chess)bookseller or at newinchess.com | a **NEW IN CHESS** publication

Using the New In Chess app is easy!

- get early access to every issue
- replay all games in the Gameviewer

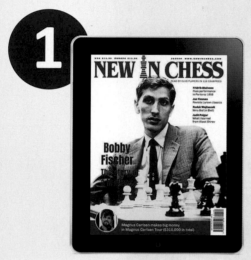

Sign in with your username and password to access the digital issue.

Read the article, optimized for your screen size.

Click on the Gameviewer button to get to the built-in chess board.

Replay the game, including an option to analyze with Stockfish.

The chess magazine that moves

www.newinchess.com/chess-apps

Contents

'Give us back our thinking time!'

CONTRIBUTORS TO THIS ISSUE
Erwin l'Ami, Jorden van Foreest, Anish Giri, Tim Harding, John Henderson, Willy Hendriks, Vincent Keymer, Peter Heine Nielsen, Maxim Notkin, Arthur van de Oudeweetering, Judit Polgar, Alejandro Ramirez, Matthew Sadler, Han Schut, Wesley So, Jan Timman, Loek van Wely, Thomas Willemze

The Queen's Gambit

t's time for Netflix and chess as the streaming behemoth's eagerly-awaited *The Queen's Gambit* is premiered worldwide on October 23. The seven-part limited series is based on Walter Tevis's 1983 popular chess-themed novel of the same name.

Garry Kasparov acted as the consultant to the series, and he claims the chess scenes to be as close as possible to the authentic atmosphere of chess tournaments. The trailers look lush and stylish with a storyline that follows an orphan in late-1950s Kentucky named Beth Harmon. She discovers that she has an incredible talent for chess, as she walks the fine dividing line between 'genius and madness' in her consuming quest to become a grandmaster in a male-dominated world.

Anya Taylor-Joy takes on the challenging role of Beth, the skilled and glamorous outcast 'haunted by her personal demons and fuelled by a cocktail of narcotics and obsession', so says the Netflix blurb. Not only that, but the acclaimed young actress, who is quickly carving out a name for herself by playing strong-willed women, seems to have taken to chess through her new role.

'I fell in love with the game', said Taylor-Joy in a recent interview. 'I spend a lot of time in my characters' heads and that's where my research comes from for me. It's about understanding them, but obviously, when you're playing chess, you actually need to know the rules of the game and you need to know what you're talking about. So I have lots of really niche knowledge on chess now that I'm very proud of.' ∎

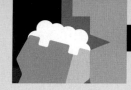

Magnus Inc.

Not content with raking in the cash with his play at the board, World Champion Magnus Carlsen is also looking to make a fortune by being 'on the board' with the biggest ever investment in a chess company, as his

Magnus Carlsen promised that he would not sacrifice the Oslo Stock Exchange.

Play Magnus Group is now listed on the Merkur Market of the Oslo Stock Exchange.

Its listing on 8 October saw Play Magnus AS (that consists of Chess24, Chessable, CoChess and the Play Magnus app) valued at approximately $120 million, although after a couple of days of trading it settled to around $100 million. Carlsen's initial investment for 60% of the company was just $13,000. Following the listing, his shareholding is today worth approximately $12 million. American asset manager Luxor Capital is now Play Magnus' largest shareholder with 10.96%.

The group's successful float raised almost $30.2 million in fresh equity, which will be used, they claim, 'for technology development and further growth.' They plan to capitalize on their own brand ambassador's continued popularity to grow the game globally, especially after the successful launch of their online Magnus Carlsen Chess Tour.

'The company has a unique vision to make chess available to new target groups all over the world,' said Carlsen on the listing. 'In addition, our model will help many more chess players and coaches to be able to make a living from chess. The company has just started on this journey and I look forward to being part of it going forward.'

Masquerade

We believed we'd heard the last of Igors Rausis after the Latvian ex-grandmaster was caught red-handed in a French toilet using a smartphone (see New In Chess 2019/6). He was subsequently stripped of his title and also handed a six-year playing ban by FIDE for his cheating.

But on social media, GM Arturs Neiksans revealed Rausis' 'comeback' in early October at the Vsevoloda Dudzinska Memorial in the Latvian capital Riga. With Covid-19 precautions in place, four-time Latvian champion Neiksans heard suspicions that one unknown and unrated competitor was the banned ex-GM playing incognito behind a mask! He immediately confronted Rausis, only to be shown a new ID card with his legal name changed to 'Isa Kasimi'.

The chief arbiter, unsure of how to proceed with the incident, put in an urgent call to one of Latvia's top arbiters... and his advice was that it was all perfectly legal with a name change for Rausis to play! That idea was not shared by the other participants, and realizing that the feeling

In Round 1 Igors Rausis (top right) cleverly used his hand as a mask.

around the playing hall was turning tense, the chief arbiter requested Rausis to leave the building, which he did.

Don't look down!

And here's more turmoil. The chess.com PRO Chess League season finale ended in controversy and bitter acrimony after the newly-crowned 2020 champions, the Armenia Eagles (GMs Tigran L. Petrosian, Parham Maghsoodloo, Haik Martirosyan and Raunak Sadhwani), were disqualified and stripped of the title following accusations of cheating.

The Eagles had defied the odds by beating the strong favourites in the final, the Saint Louis Archbishops (with the higher-rated US Olympiad

The finalists of the PRO Chess League were not so happy together.

stars Fabiano Caruana, Wesley So, Leinier Dominguez and Jeffery Xiong), to clinch the title and $20,000 first prize. But their celebrations soon turned sour when Wesley So strongly hinted at accusations of cheating from Petrosian, who not only beat Caruana, So, and Dominguez, but also top-scored with an undefeated 3½/4.

The claim was that throughout the match (and allegedly also against the Canada Chessbrahs in the semi-finals), Petrosian could be seen on the live video feed continually glancing downwards at something on his computer desk, the suspicions being a chess engine running on a smartphone.

After an investigation, Chess.com determined that the Armenian had violated their fair play regulations during both the semifinal and the final. Petrosian was given a lifetime ban on Chess.com and the PRO Chess League, and his team, the Armenia Eagles, were temporarily banned from participating in future PRO Chess League seasons, with the title and prize-money instead going to the Saint Louis Arch Bishops.

Whether that was the end of the drama, we'll have to see. Petrosian hit back to repudiate all the charges during a live Facebook press conference, claiming US favouritism by the organizers, and threatening legal action to clear his name.

Making the grade

It has become a long drawn-out saga as the United Kingdom gears up for its existential split with the European Union at the end of the year. Yet despite the 'taking back control' patriotic mantra from the politicos, the English Chess Federation is doing the least Brexity thing possible by replacing its old three-figure grading system to finally adopt the universal four-figure system devised by Prof. Arpad Elo.

The ECF grading system has been in operation since the 1950s when it was championed by the now-defunct British Chess Federation. In 1977, Scotland was the first to declare 'independence' by converting to the global FIDE Elo system, and a few years later, Wales & Ireland followed

England's number one Matthew Sadler: from 281 to 2808 in a day!

suit. But England stayed alone and defiant. Until now, that is.

The September 2020 ECF grading list is the first with the new ratings, and is led by Matthew Sadler on 2808 (which in July was still a measly 281!) followed by Mickey Adams on 2763 (instead of the old 275).

With the change, there's no truth to the rumour that the English-inspired '150 Attack' against the Pirc will now be known as the '1825 Attack'!

Strange times

We're told we live in strange times, and it appears to be spilling over to the elite-level game with some weird and off-beat openings. It all started when Hikaru Nakamura reprised his infamous

World Champion logic: if you vacate a square for your king...

'Bongcloud Attack' with 1.e4 e5 2.♔e2??! – that he played three times against Levon Aronian in the 2018 Chess.com Speed Chess Championship – to beat rising US junior Jeffery Xiong in the final round of the online Saint Louis Rapid & Blitz tournament. The nomenclature originated from its early ICC roots, as several kibitzers claimed that those playing it had to be smoking something a little, er, strange.

Rising to the silliness challenge next came Magnus Carlsen, who hit Wesley So with the psychological mind-blower of 1.f3 e5 2.♔f2??! in the opening game of their Chess24

Banter Series final... and then went on to win not only the game but also the match.

The World Champion explained that in Norway it's called 'the Greek', while others claim it to be 'the Fried Fox Attack' or 'the Hammerschlag'.

And while everyone thought it was a hoot for Carlsen to be playing it, he might have been paying tribute to another World Champion! The opening shot to fame in 2001 when a still unknown prankster managed to hoodwink many in the online chess community, including Nigel Short – who was '99% sure' at the time – they were playing Bobby Fischer.

Successful Swindle

It's not often at New In Chess that we blow our own trumpet, but we're blowing our own trumpet! The reason for the horn-blowing is to congratulate David Smerdon for winning the English Chess Federation Book of the Year 2020, the award that Hans Ree recently called 'the Nobel Prize for chess literature'.

His witty, entertaining and erudite *The Complete Chess Swindler*, the jury said, '... stood out for its original subject matter, which was treated in a serious manner, but with good writing and a considerable sense of humour.'

The mastery of this evil art in chess can be a very potent weapon, and one that players of all strengths have come to love, laugh, despise, swear and cry over. Have you ever experienced any

of those swindling emotions? If so, you can win 250 Euro in our NIC Swindle Award by sending your great escape to swindles@newinchess.com (before December 31, 2020). Award-winning author David Smerdon will judge the best Swindle of 2020. ∎

On the Origin of Good Moves

Willy Hendriks has indeed done it again (Darwin Plays Chess, New In Chess 2020/5), providing thought-provoking prose that combines chess with philosophy/metaphysics.

At the risk of sounding foolish and/or from another, earlier era, I've always had problems with the theory of bottom-up evolution and the notion that consciousness rose from inert matter. I recall seeing a museum film as a kid depicting some stray lightning bolt striking the ocean and just happening to create simple, self-replicating cellular life and from there protozoan, molluscs, fish, sharks, whales, insects, lizards, birds, apes, humans. That seemed rather far-fetched to me as did the notion that if an eye in the back of your head would be advantageous, you and enough other of your species would buck genes and have offspring born with eyes in the back of their heads so as to make that trait the new norm.

More likely to me seemed the existence of some supervising intelligence directing the development and evolution of life. Some respected non-deist groups have called such an incorporeal intelligence foundation consciousness.

In chess, there is no doubt that such supervising intelligence exists. In fact, quite a large and diverse collection of supervising intelligences. These intelligences not only found the good moves in the first place, but decided how those good moves might be fit together into strategic schemes for winning chess games against skilled rival intelligences. Some intelligences decided to use good moves to develop systems for attacking the rival's king. Others used them to achieve winning endgames in which their rivals often did not even realize they were lost until they were well underway. Modern chess intelligences pick and choose from a variety of established styles and systems, devising ever more subtle winning ways. While I suppose that this picking, choosing and refining could be characterized as bottom-up evolution, it could equally be viewed as directed development and evolution supervised by the various pre-existing intelligences involved (a fair number of which these days existing without animal bodies!).

The Benko-Botvinnik example does indeed confirm that 'history is written by the victors'. Hence one must consult English Opening texts to read that in opposition to Botvinnik's 'winning strategy' of weakening and winning White's kingside pawns was Benko's winning strategy of advancing those pawns to pry open, attack and checkmate Black's king. Alas, as Mr. Hendriks himself notes, the triumph of the latter's winning strategy only occurred in annotations, leaving to other supervising intelligences the task of finding and building on Benko's winning strategy.

Wayne R. Gradl
Getzville, New York, USA

All rook endings are drawn?

Not all rook endings are drawn, but they definitely have a large drawish tendency as witness the game between Bobby Fischer and Fridrik Olafsson that features in the article 'Peaking in Portoroz' in New In Chess 2020/6. Fischer missed several defences and in his analysis Helgi Olafsson also missed the first.

Olafsson-Fischer
Portoroz interzonal 1958 (1)
position after 32.f5

In this position Black played:
32...♖c7? Fischer and Olafsson missed the defence 32...♔f8!, when the resulting rook endings are drawn:

– 33.♗xe6 ♖xe6 34.fxe6 ♖c7 35.♖f1+ (35.♖d7 ♖c2=) 35...♔e8=.
– 33.♖d6 exf5 34.♗xf7 ♔xf7 35.♖f6+ ♔g7 36.♖xf5 b5=.

33.♖d6! Of course not the direct 33.♗xe6+? ♖xe6 34.fxe6 (after 34.fxe6 Olafsson concludes: 'White has three pawns on the e-file and they are not going anywhere') 34...♔f8 which transposes to 32...♔f8!.

33...♖c5 Now 33...♔f8 can be met by 34.♗a4+−. **34.♗xe6+ ♔f8**

35.♗b3? This wastes precious time. The direct 35.♗d5! ♖xe5 36.e4 ♖cxd5 37.exd5 ♖e4 38.♖xh6 ♖xg4 39.♖h7 ♖d4 40.♖xb7 a6 (the move given

COLOPHON

PUBLISHER: Allard Hoogland
EDITOR-IN-CHIEF:
Dirk Jan ten Geuzendam
HONORARY EDITOR: Jan Timman
CONTRIBUTING EDITOR: Anish Giri
EDITORS: Peter Boel, René Olthof
PRODUCTION: Joop de Groot
TRANSLATOR: Piet Verhagen
SALES AND ADVERTISING: Remmelt Otten

PHOTOS AND ILLUSTRATIONS IN THIS ISSUE:
Alina I'Ami, Rob Bogaerts, Christian Bossert, Collection David DeLucia, Joost Evers, Lotis Key, Lennart Ootes, Berend Vonk, Michael Zahn

COVER DESIGN: Hélène Bergmans

© No part of this magazine may be reproduced, stored in a retrieval system or transmitted in any form or by any means, recording or otherwise, without the prior permission of the publisher.

NEW IN CHESS
P.O. BOX 1093
1810 KB ALKMAAR
THE NETHERLANDS

PHONE: 00-31-(0)72-51 27 137
SUBSCRIPTIONS: nic@newinchess.com
EDITORS: editors@newinchess.com
ADVERTISING: otten@newinchess.com

WWW.NEWINCHESS.COM

by Olafsson; White also wins after 40...♖xd5 41.♖xa7 ♖xf5 42.♔h2!) is indeed better and wins, e.g. 41.♖d7 a5 42.d6 ♔e8 43.♖g7 ♖xd6 44.♖xg5 ♖d2 45.♖g7 ♖xa2 46.♖a7!.

35...♖cxe5 36.♖xh6 ♖xe3 37.♖g6 ♖8e4?! Easier is the direct 37...♖xb3! 38.axb3 ♖e3 39.♖xg5 ♖xb3 with a draw, as given by Olafsson.

38.♖xg5

38...♖g3? This is the final mistake. Black should have played 38...♖f4! 39.♔h2 ♖f2 and now:

– 40.♖g6. Olafsson: 'Black faces a near impossible defence'. But with computer help Black should be able to survive, e.g. 40...b5 41.f6 ♖xb3 42.axb3 ♔f7 43.♖h6 ♖xf6 44.♖h7+ ♔g6 45.♖xa7 ♖f4 46.♖d7 ♖xg4 with a draw.

– 40.♖g8+ ♔e7 41.♖g7+ ♔f6 42.♖g6+ ♔e7 43.♗d5 b5 44.♖a6 ♖d3 45.♗e6 ♖d6 46.♖xa7+ ♔f6 47.♔g3 ♖fd2 with a draw.

39.♖g8+ ♔e7 40.g5 ♖e2 41.♗d5 ♔d6 42.♗f3 ♖xa2 43.f6 ♔e6 44.♖e8+ Black resigned.

Karsten Müller
Hamburg, Germany

True insights

In the 1970s and 80s, before the computer age, the USSR was the capital of chess and held a special aura of excellence. I studied the games of Mikhail Botvinnik, Mikhail Tal and Vasily Smyslov on a daily basis. Unfortunately, information and accounts of their lives were shielded by Soviet Propaganda. In the 1990s, I had the pleasure of defeating the likes of Eduard Gufeld and Anatoly Lein in American Swiss events. Little did they know that I had studied their games from the USSR championships while wondering about their lives.

I loved the article by Alexander Münninghoff, 'Perfume for Klara Shagenovna' in New In Chess 2020/4 and I would like to thank you for it. The photos, interviews (Botvinnik), and authentic account give the reader a true insight into the lives of these great chess players while under Soviet rule.

FM Gregg Small
Beverly Hills, CA, USA

Write to us
New In Chess, P.O. Box 1093
1810 KB Alkmaar, The Netherlands
or e-mail: editors@newinchess.com
Letters may be edited or abridged

Correspondence chess anyone?

When you want to get better at chess, you need to see examples of high quality chess. Examples of beautiful combinations and examples of deep strategic ideas. And for those high quality games you study the games of the world's best players. Now you can argue that the highest quality chess today is not produced by human players, the chess engine plays much better than humans. But you will learn very little from the engine games, the problem is that games produced by engines like Stockfish are completely random. Stockfish is a brilliant tactician, but it is completely dumb in strategy. It might come as a surprise to many people, but it is true. This is the reason why the tactically relatively weak AlphaZero chess engine was able to beat it, but AlphaZero was good at strategy. Not surprisingly, a book on AlphaZero games was published.

But long before AlphaZero shook the chess world, the highest quality chess games were already there. Both tactics and a strategy, a perfect combination of both worlds. And it was produced in Correspondence Chess. To win in Correspondence Chess at the highest level you have to play perfect chess. That's where the highest quality chess games are and you can learn from it.

Unfortunately, this is virtually unknown to the general public. You can count the books published about correspondence chess on your fingers. You will have a hard time to find a single commented game on correspondence chess. You will have a hard time to find any news about ICCF tournaments. If you ask a general member of the chess community to name you the chess World Champions he most likely will name all of them to you. But if you will ask him to name a single Correspondence World Champion he most likely will not be able to do that.

In the modern chess community correspondence chess is misunderstood. There is often a bias against it, which unfortunately goes for the chess elite as well. Correspondence chess is not beyond human understanding. There are many examples of crystal-clear strategy and profoundly deep tactics, which chess engines could not find.

It was said that chess is a combination of Science, Art, and Sport. But today at the highest level it is almost only a sport. But the Science and Art side of chess is still there, in correspondence chess, but it is lost for the wider chess community.

Kirill Oseledets,
Chicago, IL. USA

Editorial postscript:

It is true that correspondence chess is largely ignored by the wider chess community, most probably because of the high level you mention and the complexity of the games. These games are certainly not overlooked by the stronger players, however, who closely follow the latest developments in correspondence chess. In the New In Chess Yearbook, GM Erwin l'Ami has a highly entertaining column about correspondence chess to keep the interested club player informed. ■

Third Norway Chess win for Carlsen

... but his unbeaten streak in classical chess ends after 125 games

Magnus Carlsen and Levon Aronian happily stick to the ritual of saying *namaste* at the start of the last round.

They were quarantined for 10 days, and then six GMs sat down at the boards for a memorable 8th edition of Altibox Norway Chess. Magnus Carlsen was critical about his return to 'the wooden screen', as he wittily dubbed it, but even 'pretty clueless', the World Champion was too formidable a force for the others, including a sensational Alireza Firouzja. Report by **DIRK JAN TEN GEUZENDAM**.

Levon Aronian came up with the idea at the players' meeting, and Magnus Carlsen immediately embraced it. How do you greet your opponent when you're not supposed to shake hands? The Armenian grandmaster suggested an Indian *namaste*, a slight inclination of the head with the palms of your hands pressed together and your fingers pointing upwards. Why this peaceful gesture appealed to the fighter Carlsen we don't know – a suggestion to see chess as a martial art form? – but he faithfully stuck to it all through the event.

Everything was different in this unique edition of Altibox Norway Chess, of course. To begin with, players, their companions and foreign staff members arrived 10 days in advance to undergo quarantine in the Clarion Hotel. Only after having tested negative for Covid-19 at the end of this period were they given access to the hotel's restaurant and gym. Once the players could move around freely, life became fairly normal, except for the social distancing and sanitizing that has become common everywhere. This also included clear restrictions for visitors and guests, who were virtually absent as a result.

Due to international travel restrictions, the number of participants was reduced from the usual ten players to six: two from Norway, three from other European countries and one American – Fabiano Caruana, who also holds an Italian passport. No Chinese this time and no Russians, because it simply was not possible. The result was a mix of world stars and up-and-coming stars, which turned out to be a blessing in disguise.

In the past few years, Norway Chess always aimed for having as many world top-10 players as possible in order to substantiate their claim of being 'the world's strongest tournament'. But inviting only the elite does not always guarantee the most attractive chess. This time, the differences in

Last year, less than 25 per cent of the games were decided – often because players intentionally steered for the Armageddon tiebreaker – while this time 60(!) per cent of the games saw a decision

strength and the presence of a couple of swashbucklers led to lots of entertaining clashes and a sharp increase in decisive games and the excitement that comes with them. Last year, less than 25 per cent of the games were decided – often because players intentionally steered for the Armageddon tiebreaker – while this time 60(!) per cent of the games saw a decision.

One important reason why the players were more ambitious in the classical games may have been the change in the scoring system that

made going for an Armageddon game less inviting. In 2019, Magnus Carlsen won only two 'regular' games and was happy to play an Armageddon decider eight(!) times – a preference that was hard to argue with, since a classical win was worth two points and an Armageddon only slightly less – 1½ points. In the tiebreak games, he was so ruthless that they essentially won him the tournament. Fortunately – and wholeheartedly supported by the players themselves – that was altered to three points for a classical win and just one point for an Armageddon win; with the hoped-for effect.

Chess as a TV sport
The commentators for the official international broadcast were Judit Polgar and Vladimir Kramnik, working from their homes in, respectively, Budapest and Geneva. Their conversations and analysis were highly appreciated, and rightly so. Yet the numbers – hovering between six and nine K – were relatively modest, because many less chess-savvy viewers preferred their favourite streamers on other platforms.

TV2 anchor Fin Gnatt in conversation with Magnus Carlsen, Jon Ludvig Hammer and Nils Grandelius. Chess keeps doing well as a TV sport in Norway.

LENNART OOTES

The Norwegian television viewer was once again served by TV2. With their studio in Hotel Clarion, anchor Fin Gnatt and main chess expert Jon Ludvig Hammer followed the action live. They, too, had to work with far fewer guests, but interest in Norway remains considerable, thanks to the way these broadcasts make chess easily understandable for viewers with little knowledge of the game. On one of the final days, Play Magnus Group announced that NRK and TV2 had purchased the Norwegian TV rights to the upcoming online Champions Chess Tour – a remarkable example of cooperation between two rival networks and further proof of the continued interest in chess in Carlsen's home country, especially with so many sports hit by postponements and cancellations. Their declared ambition is 'to further develop chess as a TV sport'.

Without a plexiglass screen

The eighth edition of Norway Chess will be remembered for the unusual circumstances that the pandemic imposed, but also for an abundance of riveting chess. Everyone was so happy to be sitting at the board again – without a plexiglass screen between them, even!

Half of the field consisted of previous winners: Magnus Carlsen (2016 and 2019), Fabiano Caruana (2018) and Levon Aronian (2017). Caruana may have hesitated to accept the invitation, since the second half of the Candidates Tournament was scheduled to start less than two weeks after Norway Chess. In the end, his desire to play and the uncertainty about the Candidates must have made it a fairly easy choice. And it was the correct choice, too, he must have thought when the news broke that the Candidates had been postponed again, this time till the spring of 2021.

Levon Aronian was happy to be back in Stavanger, evincing his hunger to play with four wins and an Elo gain of 14.4 points, which saw

The sensation of the tournament, 17-year-old Alireza Firouzja, gained 20.6 rating points and is now number 17 in the world

him rise from 9th to 6th place in the world rankings. When he was not playing, Aronian closely followed the escalating conflict between Azerbaijan and Armenia about Nagorno-Karabakh, a crisis that visibly affected him.

The biggest Elo gain was made by the sensation of the tournament, 17-year-old Alireza Firouzja, who finished in second place. The Iranian-born Parisian, who now plays under the FIDE flag, added 20.6 points to his total and is now number 17 in the world, with a rating of 2749.

In the first round, Firouzja beat Poland's Jan-Krzysztof Duda, who never shies away from a fight either. Duda replaced Anish Giri. The Dutchman had declined the invitation because of worries about the pandemic.

NOTES BY Jan Timman

**Jan-Krzysztof Duda
Alireza Firouzja**
Stavanger 2020 (1)
Caro-Kann, Classical Variation

1.e4 c6

It was to be expected that Firouzja would go for the Caro-Kann, which he had played four times in the St. Louis Rapid and Blitz. In this light, Duda's comment afterwards was quite remarkable: 'I was surprised by the Caro-Kann. I didn't expect it. My coach expected it, but I didn't listen to him and paid the price.'

2.d4 d5 3.♘c3 dxe4 4.♘xe4 ♗f5 5.♘g3 ♗g6 6.h4 h6 7.♘f3 ♘d7 8.h5 ♗h7 9.♗d3 ♗xd3 10.♕xd3 e6 11.♗d2 ♘gf6 12.0-0-0 ♗e7 13.♔b1 0-0 14.♘e4 c5

An over-familiar position, which has been seen frequently in practice. But to Duda it wasn't familiar territory. He thought for 33 minutes here.
15.♗e3 'Very passive,' Firouzja observed afterwards. Yet strong grandmasters like Beliavsky and McShane have played this move before. Not that Duda seemed to know this. Either way, the text does not yield him any advantage.
The critical move is 15.g4. This has also been seen in many games. The continuation is 15...♘xg4 16.♕e2 ♕b6 17.♘e5 ♘dxe5 18.dxe5 f5, and now White can take *en passant* or withdraw the knight to c3, in both cases with sufficient compensation for the pawn, but not more.
15...♘xe4 The alternative 15...♕c7 has also been played a few times, but the text is sharper.
16.♕xe4 ♘f6 17.♕xb7

Yes, in for a penny, in for a pound, however dangerous it looks. Withdrawing his queen is tantamount to handing Black the initiative on a platter.

17...♘d5 Another sharp move; but 17...♖b8, chasing back the queen, would have been more accurate. After 18.♕a6 ♕c7 Black has excellent compensation for the pawn.

18.♕a6 White could have struck with 18.dxc5, the point being that White gives his queen: 18...♘c3+ 19.bxc3! ♖b8 20.♕b3!, and White gets a super-solid structure on the queenside. After 20...♖xb3+ 21.axb3 Black has two queen moves:
– 21...♕c7 22.♖d4 ♕xc5 23.♖d7 ♕a3, and White can force move repetition with 24.♗c1, or play for a win with 24.♘e5, but he has no advantage.
– 21...♕a5 22.♘e5 ♖c8 23.♘d7 ♖c7 24.♖d3 (24.c4 can be met by 24...♕b4) 24...♖c6 (threatening 25...♖a6) 25.♘b8 ♖c8 26.♘d7, with repetition.

18...♖b8 Firouzja is trying to win an exchange, but that's a risky undertaking. More cautious was 18...♕c7, with sufficient compensation for the black pawn after 19.dxc5 ♘xe3 20.fxe3 ♕xc5 21.♘d4 ♗f6.

19.♗d2 Duda thought about this for

Only moves ago he was still fine and now Jan-Krzysztof Duda realizes that he is in big trouble as Alireza Firouzja is about to push 47...e4 with a lethal pawn storm.

just three minutes. If he had studied the position a bit more closely, he would probably have hit on the idea of offering an exchange with 19.dxc5. The white majority grows strong after 19...♘c3+ 20.♔c1 ♕c8 21.♖c4! ♘xd1 22.♖xd1, e.g. 22...♕c6 23.♘e5 ♕b7 24.b3 ♖fd8 25.♖xd8+ ♖xd8 26.f3, and Black has insufficient counterplay.

19...cxd4
An obvious move, but it has the drawback that White can now mobilize his knight for the defence. Better was the immediate 19...♗f6, with the possible continuation 20.c4 ♘b4 21.♗xb4 ♖xb4 22.♖d3 ♕a8, and Black has a very strong attack.
20.♘xd4 ♗f6 21.♘b3 ♕c7
22.♖he1 ♖fc8

23.♖c1
A better defence was 23.♕d3. Star analysts Judit Polgar and Kramnik now showed the following beautiful line: 23...a5 24.♗xa5 ♕xa5! 25.♘xa5 ♖xb2+ 26.♔c1 ♖xa2, and Black has a dangerous-looking attack. But White can save his skin with 27.c4 ♖xa5 28.♕b3, and mate has been averted. Things remain unpleasant for White after 28...♖ac5, though. The c-pawn will be lost, and Black keeps a strong initiative. He can, for example, regain the exchange whenever he wants. The computer sees little advantage for Black, but this is deceptive.
23...♘b6 24.♖e4

24...♘c4! Strange but true: this

The number of participants was reduced and there were few spectators on site but Norway Chess 2020 took place and what a celebration of chess it was!

is a theoretical novelty. Despite having arisen after inaccuracies from both sides, the position after White's 24th move already occurred in Beliavsky-Gyimesi, Bled Open 2002. In that game, Black played the inferior 24...♕c6. There followed 25.♖b4 ♕xg2 26.♕xa7 ♕xf2 27.a4 ♗xb2 28.♖f4, and now Black should have gone 28...♕g3! (instead of 28...♕e2). After 29.♔xb2 ♘c4+ 30.♖xc4 ♖xc4 31.♕e3 the position is equal. Firouzja's move is far stronger. **25.♗f4** The only try. **25...♕b6** Strong play again. Firouzja has seen that his attack will continue after the queen swap.
26.♕xb6 ♖xb6

27.♗e3
Even if White relies on the activity

of his pieces, he will be unable to prevent falling decisively behind, e.g. 27.♖d1 ♘xb2 28.♖d7 ♖b5 29.g4 a5 30.a4 ♖d5! 31.♖c7 ♖xc7 32.♗xc7 ♘d1!, and the attack continues.
27...♖b4 28.f3
Played after nearly 15 minutes of thinking. Now Duda had only seven minutes left for the rest of the game. Firouzja had 25.
White could also have sacrificed the exchange at once, but his wouldn't have solved his problems either. After 28.♖xc4 ♖bxc4 29.g3 ♘4c7 Black is winning.
28...a5 29.♖xc4 ♖cxc4 30.♗d2 ♖b5 31.♗xa5 ♖xh5 32.♖g1

32...♖b5
Hesitant play. With 32...♖ch4 Black could have aimed for a rook swap,

guaranteeing him a simple win, because the white pawns are not far enough advanced.
32...♖g5, preserving the pressure on the white g-pawn, would also have won, e.g. 33.♗d2 ♖g6 34.♘a5 ♖c8, and the white majority is too slow.
33.♗d2 h5 34.c3 g5 35.♔c2 g4 36.♘c1

36...g3
A curious move. There was nothing against the obvious 36...gxf3 37.gxf3+ ♔h7, creating a dangerous passed h-pawn that will end up deciding the issue. After the text White will be able to block the black majority for a considerable time.
37.b3 ♖c8 38.a4 ♖f5 39.♘e2 h4 40.c4

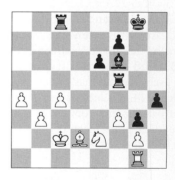

40...e5 Another mistake, which throws away all Black's advantage. With 40...♔f8 he could have directed his king to the queenside. A possible continuation was 41.♖h1 ♔e8 42.♘c3 ♔d7 43.♘e4 ♗e7, and Black has winning chances.
41.♗e3
Duda plays excellently during this part of the game. The alternative 41.♗e1 was less accurate, since

41...♖h5 42.♖h1 ♖h7 could have given Black some winning chances. **41...♗g5 42.♗xg5 ♖xg5 43.♖h1 ♖h5**

Around this time, Firouzja must have offered a draw; I have not been able to ascertain exactly when. Both players were already on increments anyway. Duda refused. As it turned out, he had been very optimistic about his chances. Afterwards he even said that he thought he had been winning at some point. That is completely untrue. In this part of the game, the position was dynamically balanced.

44.♔c3 A sign of optimism. With 44.♘xg3 White could more or less have forced a draw. After 44...♖g5 45.♘e4 ♖xg2+ 46.♔c3 ♖g6 47.♖xh4 f5 48.♘d2 chances are equal.

44...f5 45.b4 f4

46.a5

A serious error, as Firouzja will demonstrate convincingly. White had two ways to maintain the balance. With 46.♘g1 he could try to block the pawn majority. But it's not a complete blockade, since Black can crash through with 46...♖d8 47.♘h3, and now 47...e4!. Black will end up with too few pawns to win, e.g. 48.fxe4 ♖f8 49.♖f1 f3 50.♖xf3 ♖xf3+ 51.gxf3 g2 52.a5 ♖h6 53.c5 ♔g7 54.♔d2 ♖g6 55.c6 ♖xc6 56.♔e3, and the draw is in sight.

46.b5 was also sufficient for a draw. In these kinds of positions, it is usually best to start advancing the passed pawn in the middle. Here is a long and virtually forced line to illustrate this: 46...h3 47.♖xh3 ♖xh3 48.gxh3 e4 49.♘g1! ♖d8 50.b6 ♔f7 51.a5 ♖d3+ 52.♔c2 exf3 53.b7 f2 54.b8♕ fxg1♕ 55.♕xf4+, and a draw by perpetual check.

After the game Duda suggested that he could also have blocked the black majority with 46.♖h3, but this is insufficient, since Black could have broken through with his e- and f-pawns, after which the white rook would have been badly positioned: 46...e4! 47.fxe4 f3! 48.gxf3 g2:

ANALYSIS DIAGRAM

– 49.b5 ♔f7! 50.♔b4 (of 50.♘g1 ♖hc5) 50...♖d8, and the rook penetrates.
– 49.♖h2 h3 50.a5 ♔f7 51.♘g1 ♖d8, with the same outcome.

46...h3!

47.gxh3

47.♖xh3 would have given better practical chances.

After 47...♖xh3 48.gxh3 Firouzja would have too little time to find a win. Let's have a look:

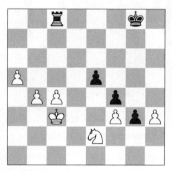

ANALYSIS DIAGRAM

– 48...e4 49.♘g1! exf3 50.♘xf3 ♖a8 (after 50...♖e8 White saves himself with 51.a6) 51.b5! ♖xa5 52.b6, and Black cannot win – the white b-pawn is too strong.

– 48...♖a8!. This is the only way Black will be able to claim the game. He temporarily stops the a-pawn, while preparing the decisive breakthrough. After 49.b5 (or 49.c5 ♔f7 50.♔c4 ♔e6, and the rook penetrates via the d-file) 49...e4! 50.♘g1 ♖xa5 51.b6 ♖a1 White is left empty-handed. By postponing the breakthrough of the e-pawn, Black could have restricted White's elbow-room in this line.

47...e4

The second breakthrough, which is decisive here.

48.fxe4 g2 49.♖g1 ♖xh3+ 50.♔d4 f3 51.c5 ♔f7 52.♘f4 f2

White resigned.

∎ ∎ ∎

After three rounds Aronian and Caruana were tied for the lead. Round 4 brought the big clash between Carlsen and Caruana. In their previous 19 classical games, the World Champion had not been able to defeat his closest rival.

NOTES BY
Anish Giri

Magnus Carlsen
Fabiano Caruana
Stavanger 2020 (4)
Nimzo-Indian Defence, Classical Variation

1.d4 ♘f6 2.c4 e6 3.♘c3 ♗b4 4.♕c2

The ♕c2 Nimzo used to be a frequent guest in Magnus Carlsen's games, but it's been a while since he last played it, so it may have caught Fabiano Caruana somewhat off guard.

4...0-0 5.a3

Fabiano himself has played 5.e4!? against Magnus. The main move 5.a3 is considered even more harmless by modern chess theory, but the element of surprise is crucial.

5...♗xc3+ 6.♕xc3 d5

Ever since Vladimir Kramnik introduced 7.cxd5 ♘e4! – an important finesse that this line is based on – the move 6...d5 has become the main line, and the traditional 6...b6 has moved into the shadows.

7.♗g5

This move is trendy every now and then.

7...dxc4

The alternative 7...c5!? leads to fascinating positions, while the text-move looks somewhat more reliable. In the ♕c2 Nimzo White generally has the bishop pair, but as a rule, Black strikes first in the centre in hopes of getting ahead in development, while White is wasting time with all his queen moves.

8.♕xc4 b6 9.♖d1 ♗a6 10.♕a4 h6 11.♗h4

11...♕d7

Fishing for an endgame is a reliable way of playing this position, but the verdict of this line is not entirely certain yet, since some people argue White retains a small plus. I myself have played the move 11...♕e7 here, followed by ...♖d8 and ...c5, but I am sure Magnus wanted to ask some questions there, too.

12.♕c2 ♕c6

I find this too desperate, but then again, it does simplify the game.

13.♕xc6 ♘xc6 14.♗xf6

White cashes out his bishop pair, but instead gains another long-term asset: a slightly better pawn structure. The doubled f-pawns aren't a big deal, but could be an issue, as in the classic

For 19 classical games Magnus Carlsen had not been able to defeat Fabiano Caruana. Now the full point was his, as the American suddenly slipped up in a defendable position.

22.♘c6. Very minor issues, but still...
21.dxc5 bxc5 22.♖c2

22...♔f8
Strangely enough, this neutral move, bringing the king closer to the d6-knight and intending to meet 23.♖d1 with 23...♔e7, turns out to be very unfortunate. If Fabi had started with 22...♖ab8 and ...c4 here, I think he would have managed. This move is not so bad in itself, but as we will see later, it creates an important nuance. 22...♖ab8 23.♘d2 (23.♖d1 might have bothered Fabi, but it is not a big deal after 23...♖b6) 23...c4 24.♖bc1 ♔g7 25.♔f3 (this would be the same position as in the game, but with the king on g7 instead of f8) 25...c3 26.bxc3 ♘c4

ANALYSIS DIAGRAM

would be a relatively easy draw, as after 27.♘xc4 ♖xc4 28.♖d1 the penetration of the rooks to the 7th is less painful: 28...♖b3 29.♖d7 ♖xa3 30.♖b2, and with the king on g7 and not on f8, there is 30...♖c8! 31.♖bb7 ♖f8!, and the c-pawn will eventually be traded for the a-pawn. With pawns on only one wing there is no danger.
23.♘d2 c4 24.♖bc1

Cohn-Rubinstein game and the more recent Salem-Kramnik from Qatar a few years back – games you should look up if you ever want to flex, like I did just now.

14...gxf6 15.e3 ♗xf1
It is also typical to play 15...♗b7!? here, intending ...♖fc8/...♘e7, eventually followed by the liberating ...c5 push. I remembered I was impressed when Leko played this move against me in a similar position. It looks so classy!
16.♔xf1 ♘a5 17.♘f3
Actually, so far we have been following

Wang Hao-Radjabov from the Online Nations Cup this year.

17...♘c4 A fine-looking move. Radjabov went for 17...♖ac8 and ...c5, but I guess 17...♖fc8 and ...c5, in whatever order, is fine too.
18.♖b1 c5 19.♔e2 ♖fc8 20.♖hc1 ♘d6
The knight has made it to a reasonable square. Fabiano could trade the c-pawn without creating a weakness, but there would be some minor technical difficulties due to the slightly weakened c6-square and the doubled f-pawns: 20...cxd4 21.♘xd4 ♘d6

24...♖ab8

24...♖cb8!? was another way to defend, the idea being that Black gets out of a potential x-ray on the c-file, not allowing any b4 intermezzos: 25.♔f3 ♔g7 26.♘xc4 ♘xc4 27.♖xc4 ♖xb2, and this should be not much for White.

25.♔f3 c3

I suspect Fabi played this intending to follow it up with ...♘c4, but then noticed 28.♖d1! down the line and was forced to change his mind.

– 25...f5 was a reasonable attempt to try and defend: 26.♘xc4 ♖xc4 27.♖xc4 ♘xc4 28.♖xc4 ♖xb2 29.♖c7 f4!? 30.♖xa7 fxe3 31.fxe3, and such an endgame must be within the drawing margins, although it wouldn't be much fun, especially since White's king has an excellent starting point on f3 to join the queenside pawn (with the king is cut off on g2, it is usually a trivial draw).

– 25...♖c5, with the idea of 26.b4! ♖c6!, is the engine's solution, since 27.♘xc4 is met by 27...♖bc8, but for humans it is quite hard to see beyond the pretty 26.b4! shot.

26.bxc3

26...♖c5

After 26...♘c4, 27.♘xc4 ♖xc4 28.♖d1!

ANALYSIS DIAGRAM

is incredibly nasty, with the looming invasion ♖d7: 28...♖a4 (28...♖b7, guarding the 7th, allows 29.♖d4!, gaining more ground, and 28...♖b3 won't work: 29.♖d7 ♖xa3 30.♖b2, with the second rook invading the 7th) 29.♖d7 ♖xa3 30.c4. This is very unpleasant with the c-pawn running down the board and the 7th-rank issues unresolved.

27.c4 Now, although Black does have some drawing chances, he is really a pawn down.

27...f5 28.♔e2 ♔e7 29.♔d3

The king comes closer to the c4-pawn, freeing one of White's pieces from defending it.

29...♔d7 30.♖c3

Intending ♖b3, further improving the position.

The traditional handshake was soon forgotten once the players discovered alternatives to greet their opponent at the start of the game.

BEREND VONK

30...♖c6? Fabiano must have overlooked something, because allowing c5 is a disaster. There was no draw or clear-cut defence available here, and a neutral waiting move (e.g. ...♔e7) would have been far better.
31.c5! ♘e8 32.♘f3!

Now White is winning. The c-pawn is no longer weak, but all of a sudden very, very strong.
32...♖a6 33.♘e5+ ♔e7 34.♔e2
In full control, Magnus regroups his pieces. 34.♔c2!, intending ♖b1 or ♖b3, was also strong.
34...♘f6 35.♖1c2 ♘d5 36.♖d3

White is guarding all his pawns and vital squares.
36...♖c8 37.♖b3 ♖c7 38.♖c4 ♖a5 39.♘d3

Fabiano must have overlooked something, because allowing c5 is a disaster

39...e5? Black's position feels hopeless, but this only speeds things up. Fabiano must have missed a nuance in the end.
40.♘xe5 ♖axc5 41.♖xc5 ♖xc5 42.♖b7+ ♔e6 43.♘xf7 ♖a5
Maybe Fabiano intended 43...♖c2+ 44.♔f3 ♘f6

ANALYSIS DIAGRAM

with some ...♘e4 illusions, but there is a harsh refutation: 45.♘xh6! ♘e4 46.♘xf5! ♔xf5 47.g4+!, and wins.
44.♘d8+ ♔d6 45.♖b3
Black has gained nothing, and only lost another pawn, so the rest is really trivial.

45...♖a6 46.♘f7+ ♔c5 47.♘e5 h5 48.♔d2 h4 49.♘d3+ ♔c4 50.♔c2 ♖d6 51.♘f4
Black resigned.

■ ■ ■

One day it would happen

With his win over Caruana, Carlsen not only moved into first place, but also extended his unbeaten streak in classical chess to 125 games. His next opponent was Jan-Krzysztof Duda, who was having a tough time. He had lost his first three games, and after a draw against Aryan Tari in Round 4 he had slipped up in the Armageddon game.

NOTES BY
Erwin l'Ami

Jan-Krzysztof Duda
Magnus Carlsen
Stavanger 2020 (5)
Caro-Kann, Kortchnoi Variation

1.e4 c6 2.d4 d5 3.♘c3 dxe4 4.♘xe4 ♘f6

This move has recently gained in popularity and may soon replace 4...♗f5 as the main move in this line of the Caro-Kann.

5.♘xf6+ exf6

The best way to recapture. Yes, if we now remove all pieces from the board, White will win the pawn ending, but this is merely an abstract thought, since Black is unlikely to cooperate. For now, Black's kingside structure makes for a very safe king after kingside castling, and the f6-pawn is taking away a couple of key squares (e5 and g5) from White's pieces.

Viktor Kortchnoi used this variation multiple times, e.g. in his 1978 World Championship match against Anatoly Karpov. This is why the variation justifiedly carries his name.

6.c3 ♗d6 7.♗d3 0-0 8.♕c2 ♖e8+ 9.♘e2

White has many different set-ups but Duda's is generally considered the most venomous one. What's more, for a long time this setup was thought to make Black's entire approach look at best dubious.

9...h5! This pawn move has breathed new life into the line. The pawn is not so much of a target on h5 if White castles queenside, but if he castles the other way, it will be quite annoying once it goes ...h4-h3.

10.♗e3 ♘d7 11.0-0-0

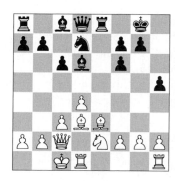

11...b5!?

In my Caro-Kann course for Chessable, I focus on 11...♘f8, mentioning the game continuation only as an interesting alternative. It is essentially a pawn sacrifice that was also played by Jorden van Foreest earlier this year. In that game, following 12.♔b1 ♘b6 13.♖he1 ♗e6, Black already had a clear advantage due to his excellent control of the light squares.

12.d5 The only way to question Black's previous move.

12...c5 13.♗xb5

13...♖b8

The position that Magnus must have envisioned when going for 11...b5. White has won a pawn, but Black gets long-term compensation with the open b-file. In the afore-mentioned course, I also considered the fascinating exchange sacrifice 13...♖xe3 14.fxe3 ♘e5. It is hard to say how correct this is, but despite Black being an exchange and a pawn down, his blockade on the dark squares, the beautiful knight on e5 and the open b-file should mean serious practical compensation.

14.c4 a6 15.♗a4 ♖e7

Logical. Carlsen unpins the knight and is ready to swing the rook over to b7 at some point.

16.♘g3

16...♘e5 Continuing the plan started on move 15. But while the exchange sacrifice was merely interesting on move 13, at this point, 16...♖xe3! 17.fxe3 ♘b6 18.♗c6 h4! 19.♘f1 ♗g4 is already more than that. Black will regroup with ...♗h5-g6, ...♗e5, ...♘c8-d6/e7, with great compensation. This means that White

would probably have done better playing 16.♖he1 to prevent this mess.
17.♘e4 17.♗d2! ♖eb7 18.b3 would have given White a large advantage, since ...♖b4 has been prevented. It is a hard move to spot, but the strength of it becomes clear immediately after the game continuation.
17...♖eb7 18.b3 ♖b4!
Now the possibility of sacrifices on a4/c4 is rearing its head.

The end of a unique streak. Having gone undefeated for an unbelievable 125 classical games, Magnus Carlsen sees that there is no way out anymore after Jan-Krzysztof Duda's 62.♕h7+.

19.♗d2
19.♘xd6 was the alternative. Now 19...♕xd6 20.♖he1 prepares ♗f4 and forces Black to act quickly. According to the engine, the following line is forced: 20...♖xa4 21.bxa4 ♖b4 22.♗f4 ♘d3+ 23.♖xd3 ♕xf4+ 24.♖ee3 ♗f5 25.g3! ♗xd3 26.♕xd3 ♕xc4+ 27.♕xc4 ♖xc4+, with an equal endgame, but I can imagine Carlsen might have tried his luck with 20...g6. The comp doesn't approve, but then, with ...♗f5 coming and clear (practical) chances against White's king, that may be irrelevant.
19...♖xa4 20.bxa4 ♗f5 21.♖de1

21...h4 Black's compensation is not of the kind that allows the position to be played so slowly. Stronger was the

more urgent 21...♘g4! 22.f3 (22.♖e2 ♗e5 prepares counterplay with ...♖b2) 22...♗xe4!, when White has no good way to recapture the bishop. Both 23.♖xe4 ♘f2 and 23.fxe4 ♗e5 24.♗c3 ♕c7 25.g3 ♗d4!? are very messy and give Black ample compensation.
22.h3
22.♖e3! was more powerful, immediately taking control of the third rank. After 22...♘g4 23.♖f3! Black is basically lost. Just like 17.♗d2, it is one of those very hard-to-spot consolidating moves.
22...♘g6 23.♖e3 ♘f4

24.g4
24.f3!, with the idea of 24...♘xg2 25.♖b3, was another good way to fight for an advantage. The game continuation allows Carlsen a very complicated chance for survival.

24...♗g6
24...hxg3! 25.fxg3 ♘h5 was a surprisingly strong resource here. If 26.g4, 26...♗xe4, followed by ...♘g3, wins back the exchange, while 26.♖g1 ♗g6! would not be easy for White either. A sample line is 27.g4 ♘f4 28.♖f1 ♗e5 29.♗c3 ♗d4 30.♖g3 ♘xd5! 31.cxd5 ♕xd5 32.♖e1 ♔h8!, preparing ...♖e8, with great compensation for the rook(!).
25.♔d1
25.f3!? was good, too, stabilizing the knight on e4. But Duda's move makes a lot of sense – preparing ♖b3 without allowing ...♘e2+-d4.

25...f5
Carlsen correctly judges the time ripe for concrete action. This pawn push won't cut it, though. The tricky engine comes up with 25...♕d7! to

stop 26.♖b3, which is now met by 26...♖xb3 27.axb3 ♘xh3!!, and Black wins. 26.f3 would be better, but now the game continuation 26...f5 gains in strength after 27.♘xd6 fxg4! 28.♘e4 gxf3, which is the kind of complications Black is looking for.

26.♘xd6 ♕xd6 27.gxf5 ♗h5+ 28.f3

Now White is clearly winning, but there is a reason Magnus got to his streak of 125 games: he tends to fight back well!

28...♕f6 29.♗c3

29.♕e4! ♕a1+ 30.♗c1 ♖b1 31.♔d2! is very convincing, but one can understand Duda's reluctance to even

calculate lines involving a queen and rook landing on the first rank.

29...♕g5 30.♕e4

Duda was running short of time here and starts to drift somewhat. 30.♖he1!, preparing ♖e8+, still wins relatively straightforwardly. In the game, Carlsen gets an unlikely chance to save the game.

30...♕g2

Here 30...♕h7! 31.d6 f6! will hold for Black. Black safeguards the king before taking active measures. For instance, 32.d7 ♖d8 33.♕e7 ♕xf5! 34.♕xd8 ♕b1+ 35.♔d2 ♕xa2+ 36.♔d1 ♕b3+ 37.♔d2 ♕a2+, with a draw by perpetual check. Needless to

say, this line is close to impossible to find for a mere human.

31.♖he1 ♕xa2 32.♕c2!

Refuting Black's queen sortie.

32...♕xc4 33.♖e8+ ♔h7

It is very important that 33...♖xe8 34.♖xe8+ ♔h7 35.♖h8+!, followed by ♗xg7+, wins the queen. This means Black that has to give up a full rook.

34.♖xb8 ♕xd5+ 35.♕d2

The remainder of the game is not very interesting. Duda was (very) short on time, and I believe that to be main reason why the game lasted for another 30 moves. There were certainly moments when Jan-Krzysztof could have wrapped things up faster, but at no point did he leave the final outcome in doubt.

35...♗xf3+ 36.♔c1 ♕xf5 37.♖e3 ♘e2+ 38.♔b2 ♘xc3 39.♕xc3 ♕f4 40.♕d3+ f5 41.♖f8 ♕b4+ 42.♔c1 ♗e4 43.♕b3 ♕d4 44.♕c3 ♕d6 45.♖f7 ♕g6 46.♖d7 ♕g1+ 47.♔b2 c4 48.♖xe4 fxe4 49.♖d4 ♕f2 50.♕d2 c3+ 51.♔xc3 ♕g3+ 52.♔b2 ♕xh3 53.♖xe4 ♕g3 54.♕d4 ♕g2+ 55.♔c3 ♕f3+ 56.♔b4 ♕f8+ 57.♔a5 ♕f5+

TORPEDO KNIGHT! UNDETERRED BY THE PANDEMIC, VLADIMIR KRAMNIK KEEPS COMING UP WITH NEW EXCITING CHESS VARIANTS.

58.♔xa6 g5 59.a5 h3 60.♖e7+ ♔g6 61.♕g7+ ♔h5 62.♕h7+ ♔g4 63.♖e4+

Black resigned. The queen is lost.

■ ■ ■

Aryan Tari had been hoping for an invitation to Norway Chess for several years. So far the organizers had declined his appeals, since they were focusing on the world top, but for this special edition, the Norwegian number two had been invited. His baptism of fire could not have been rougher, for he lost seven of his first eight games before drawing the final two. In Rounds 5 and 6, he lost to Firouzja with both colours. After that second win Firouzja moved into first place, one point ahead of Carlsen and two points ahead of Aronian.

NOTES BY
Jorden van Foreest

**Aryan Tari
Alireza Firouzja**
Stavanger 2020 (6)
Caro-Kann, Exchange Variation

I like this game, which was played between the two youngest participants in this Norway Chess edition. So far, Firouzja had been crashing through the tournament, while Aryan was having a tough time of it.
1.e4 c6
The Caro-Kann was Firouzja's weapon of choice for the tournament.
2.d4 d5 3.exd5 cxd5 4.♗d3

This move came into fashion a couple of years ago. White goes for a slow game in which he nurses a slight plus. But as we see in this game, things can always get sharp and interesting very quickly. The Panov-Botvinnik with c4 is the old main line.
4...♘f6 5.c3 ♗g4 6.♕b3 ♕c7 7.h3

7...♗d7 This withdrawing of the bishop is the safest choice, since 7...♗h5 8.g4 ♗g6 9.♗xg6 hxg6 10.g5 involves the sacrifice of a pawn.
8.♘f3 ♘c6 9.0-0 e6 10.♖e1 ♗d6

11.♗g5?!
This seems dubious. White doesn't really want to take on f6 anyway, and the bishop will soon get hit by ...f7-f6. 11.♕d1, returning the queen to the centre, makes more sense. Black is

ahead in development, but White has the edge thanks to his space advantage. One of the key ideas here is ♕e2, followed by ♘e5.

11...0-0 12.♘bd2 12.♗xf6 gxf6 would be a grave positional error, because it would open the g-file for an attack on his king and give up the bishop pair.

12...♘h5

Now we see why White's 10th move was inaccurate. ...f6 is next, and the black knight has a beautiful square on f4. Tari already has to be careful if he wants to maintain the balance.

13.♕d1 f6

13...♘f4!? would have been an attractive move as well. Since White would not have the option of ♗e3 after a possible ...f6 later, he would have to give up the bishop pair.

14.♗e3 ♘f4 15.♗f1 g5!?

True to style, Firouzja plays the position in the sharpest way possible. Black is preparing a slow but hard-to-stop attack, with a very easy position.

16.c4! The good old principle remains true in this computer era: a flank attack must be countered by a strike in the centre.

16...♔h8

Naturally Black prepares ...♖g8.

17.♖c1?!

A logical but superficial move. White simply doesn't have the time to slow-play the position. It was high time to get the queenside pawns rolling.

17.a3!, preparing b4, was called

for. Although I like Black, White is probably still ever so slightly better. Now 17...a5 seems natural, to stop b2-b4, when White has a beautiful rerouting move in the form of 18.♘b1!.

17...♖g8

Continuing the afore-mentioned plan of doubling rooks on the g-file and preparing ...g4.

18.♗xf4

Getting rid of the menacing knight is a good idea, but by no means does it scupper the black attack.

Even now, 18.a3 would still have been a very reasonable move.

18...♗xf4

19.b4?!

The white position wasn't easy to play, but after this move White is also objectively worse. I fully understand Aryan's desire to create a pawn storm of his own on the queenside, but as it turns out, the white pawns aren't really going anywhere, since they have no targets to attack.

The multi-purpose move 19.♖c3! would have kept the balance. The idea is not just to cover the third rank with the rook but, more importantly, to introduce the idea of ♘d2-b3-c5. Were Black to prevent this with ...b6, he would create a hook to attack with c4-c5, e.g. 19...♕d6 20.♘b3 b6 21.c5 ♕e7 22.g3.

19...♕d6! 20.b5 ♘e7

It is almost as if White is helping

The advice 'don't make moves on the side on which you are weaker' applies here

Black to bring his pieces closer to the white king. The knight has a beautiful square available on f5.

21.c5?

Basically the decisive mistake. Closing the centre removes any hope of counterplay and gives Black a free hand to deliver checkmate on the other side of the board.

21...♕c7 22.g3?!

The advice 'don't make moves on the side on which you are weaker' applies here. This merely helps the black attack gain momentum.

I am not sure if it would have saved White, but I like the following

Alireza Firouzja is overjoyed after one of his four wins. As Magnus Carlsen commented: 'He is so strong, he is going to be around for a long time.'

helpless in the long run: 26.fxg3 ♕xg3 27.♘g1 ♘f5 28.♕f3 ♕h4 29.c6 bxc6 30.bxc6 ♗c8. Black might look uncoordinated for a moment, but order will soon be restored after he gets in ...♗a6 and ...♖ag8. Black is winning.

26.♗xd7?

After this Firouzja doesn't give his opponent another chance.

26.dxe5! was the only way to stay in the game: 26...fxe5 (26...♗xh3? 27.exf6!) 27.♘g1, and White manages to keep his position together for the moment.

26...♕xd7 27.♘h2 ♕h3

Dark clouds are gathering around the white king, now that the entire black army is joining the attack.

28.♖g1 ♖ag8 29.♕e2 e4 30.♖c3 ♘f5 The last piece joins the attack, and a sacrifice on g3 will bring the proceedings to an end.

31.♘xe4 Desperation. **31...dxe4 32.♕xe4 ♗xg3 33.♖g2 ♖e7**

I like this final switch of the rooks to the e-file.

34.♕b1 ♖ge8 Now ...♖e1+ is unstoppable (if 35.♖c1, 35...♗xh2 36.♖xh2 ♕f3+), and so White resigned.

∎ ∎ ∎

defence from the always resourceful engines: 22.♖c3! g4 23.hxg4 ♖xg4 24.c6! (distracting the black pieces from the white king) 24...bxc6 25.bxc6 ♘xc6 26.♘e5!.

ANALYSIS DIAGRAM

A really nice shot, containing a nice trap. Now 26...fxe5 27.♕xg4 ♗xd2 seems easily winning for Black, but White suddenly launches an attack of his own: 28.♖g3 ♗h6 29.♕h4 ♗g7 30.♗d3 e4 31.♖xe4 dxe4? (31...♕d8!) 32.♕xe4. However, 26...♖xg2+!, sacrificing an exchange instead, is very strong, with Black retaining a large advantage: 27.♗xg2 fxe5, and with ...♖g8 on the cards, the white

king is very unsafe. Still, this was White's best chance.

22...g4 22...♗xg3 23.fxg3 g4 was probably winning as well, but there is no need to sacrifice anything just yet.

23.hxg4 ♖xg4 24.♗h3 ♖g7 25.♔h1

25...e5?!

It's hard to criticize Firouzja for this move, since it simply looks crushing. Nevertheless, it might have given Tari a slim chance of at least surviving the first attacking wave.

Stronger was 25...♗xg3!. I am sure both players saw this, but failed to find a clear knock-out. But it turns out there is no need for one, since White is

Positional master class

Magnus Carlsen reclaimed the lead in Round 8, when he beat Tari for the second time. In the first game, the youngster had had a promising position, only to go under in the tactical melee that Carlsen whipped up.

Aryan Tari
Magnus Carlsen
Stavanger 2020 (3)

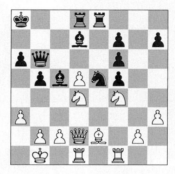

position after 22...♗d7

Carlsen's opening play has been provocative and White has a clear advantage. With 23.♕c3 or 23.d6 White could increase his pressure, but Tari believes he has time for a knight manoeuvre that only benefits Black.
23.♘h5? ♘c4 24.♗xc4 bxc4 25.♕c3 ♖b8 26.♖f3?
A further mistake. He should have continued 26.♘xf5. Now Carlsen can play a lovely move that had also been spotted by Vladimir Kramnik.

26...♖e1! In the space of a couple of moves the tables have been turned completely. **27.♖xe1 ♗xd4 28.♕b4 ♕c7 29.d6 ♕c6 30.♕a5 ♗xb2** 30...♖xb2+ was even stronger, but that's nitpicking. **31.♔a2 ♗e5**

32.♖b1 ♖xb1 33.♔xb1 ♕xd6 34.♔c1 ♕d4! 35.♕xa6+ ♔b8
And White is lost (0-1, 45).

Their second game was a positional master class.

NOTES BY
Jorden van Foreest

Magnus Carlsen
Aryan Tari
Stavanger 2020 (8)
Ruy Lopez, Modern Line

1.e4 e5 2.♘f3 ♘c6 3.♗b5 a6 4.♗a4 ♘f6 5.0-0 ♗e7 6.d3
Against 6.♖e1, Tari had prepared the Marshall Attack, and he got decent positions against both Caruana and Aronian. Carlsen clearly didn't want to venture into the forcing variations arising there and opts for a somewhat slower game instead.

6...b5 7.♗b3 d6 8.a4 ♗d7 9.c3 ♘a5 10.♗a2
A slightly surprising move, leaving the a4-pawn hanging. However, Carlsen had played this before in a rapid game versus Ding Liren.

THE NEW CHESSBASE 16 PROGRAM PACKAGES 2021 EDITION

New in ChessBase 16*

- Opening surveys for every move with a single click. With a choice of focus: Main Variations, Fashion, Side Lines, Attacking, Gambits, Endgame
- Better overview when playing through deeply analysed games thanks to dynamic folding of the notation
- Urgent news about recently played innovations with direct access to the database
- Direct database access to tournaments being played live
- Preparation for opponents with recognition of their weaknesses taking into account your own repertoire
- Innovations and trends as annotations in Tactical Analysis
- Update-Service for MegaDatabase with a single click
- After an update to Megadatabase, overview of important recent innovations and theoretical trends.
- Tags for the management of games.
- Search for characteristic tactical positions in an opening variation
- Link to the ChessBase Shop with simple installation of purchased download products
- Slimmed down search booster: required hard disk space halved
- Playchess chat modernised

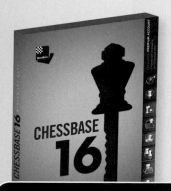

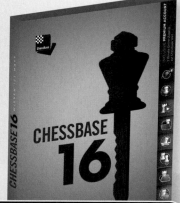

Available on DVD or as download version!

Including 500 ducats by chessbase

STARTER PACKAGE	€ 199.90	MEGA PACKAGE	€ 299.90	PREMIUM PACKAGE	€ 469.90

NEW: ChessBase 16 program

NEW: Big Database 2021

Update Service through 31.12.2021

Access to ChessBase Online Database (over 9 million games)

Subscription to ChessBase Magazine for half a year (3 issues)

ChessBase Premium membership (6 months)

NEW: ChessBase 16 program

➕ **NEW: Mega Database 2021**

Update Service through 31.12.2021

Access to ChessBase Online Database (over 9 million games)

➕ Subscription to ChessBase Magazine for a full year (6 issues)

➕ ChessBase Premium membership (12 months)

NEW: 250 ChessBase Ducats

NEW: ChessBase 16 program

➕ **NEW: Mega Database 2021**

Update Service through 31.12.2021

➕ Corr Database 2020

➕ Endgame Turbo 5 USB Stick (128 GB)

Access to ChessBase Online Database (over 9 million games)

➕ Subscription to ChessBase Magazine for a full year (6 issues)

➕ ChessBase Premium membership (12 months)

NEW: 500 ChessBase Ducats

CHESSBASE 16 UPDATE FROM CHESSBASE 15   € 99.90

*Available from 17.11.2020

Online Shop: shop.chessbase.com · ChessBase GmbH · Osterbekstr. 90a · 22083 Hamburg · Germany · info@chessbase.com
CHESSBASE DEALER: NEW IN CHESS · P.O. Box 1093 · NL-1810 KB Alkmaar · phone (+31)72 5127137 · fax (+31)72 5158234 · WWW.NEWINCHESS.COM

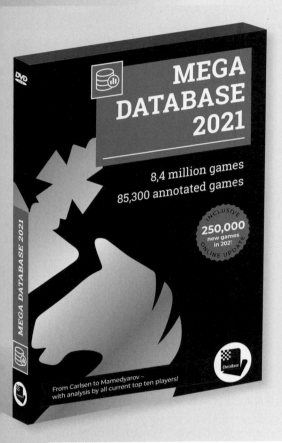
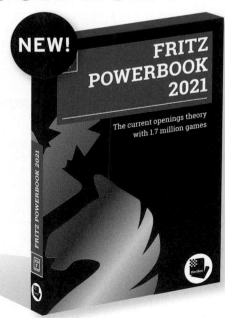

NEW FRITZ-TRAINER DVDs

Chris Ward:
SICILIAN DRAGON:
THE REAL DEAL! PART 1:
UNDERSTANDING THE DRAGON

Our new author Chris Ward starts on a small DVD series and presents in the Sicilian Dragon Variation the most aggressive reaction to 1.e4. In this first part the focus is on themes and ideas. Here you will get to know about the tactical and positional motifs and plans after 1.e4 c5 2.Nf3 d6 3.d4 cxd4 4.Nxd4 Nf6 5.Nc3 g6. From the basic weapons which are the legendary Dragon bishop and the exploitation of the c-file all the way to more complex subjects such as prophylaxis numerous subtleties are dealt with.

€ 29,90

Ivan Sokolov:
UNDERSTANDING MIDDLEGAME STRATEGIES VOL. 1 - DYNAMIC PAWNS

Many tournament and club players find strategic decisions difficult. This training course from former world class player Ivan Sokolov is about the various dynamic decisions concerning the pawns. Let the master show you ideas and techniques and employ them in your own games! The DVD's topics are divided into four chapters: "Small sacrifices", "Rolling pawns", "Allowing pawn islands", "Dynamic ideas with the g- and h-pawns".

€ 29,90

Daniel King:
POWERPLAY 28 - TACTIC TOOLBOX KING'S GAMBIT

Tactics rule in the King's Gambit. That is one reason why the opening was previously so popular and to this day still fascinates countless players. On his new DVD Daniel King presents the typical motifs and anyone who studies these tasks can be setting their opponent problems in the King's Gambit after only a few moves. And, of course, you are also guaranteed to have fun. The perfect complement to Powerplay 27 "The King's Gambit"!

€ 29,90

Ivan Sokolov:
UNDERSTANDING MIDDLEGAME STRATEGIES VOL. 2 - PRACTICAL PLAY

Learn how in the middlegame you can make better, targeted decisions and extend your understanding of the middlegame in general. This time the GM from the Netherlands uses model games to deal with the following topics: "What should you exchange and what you should keep", "The king on f8 defends itself", "Line opening", "Bringing about crises".

€ 29,90

Sergey Tiviakov:
HOW TO PLAY THE RUY LOPEZ WITH Qe2

In order to avoid theoretical battles in the main systems of the Ruy Lopez Sergey Tiviakov invites you into the world of an extraordinarily early move with the white queen: Qe2 - elegant, effective and easy to learn! The following variations are dealt with on the DVD: 1.e4 e5 2.Nf3 Nc6 3.Bb5 Nf6 4.Qe2, 3...a6 4.Ba4 Nf6 5.Qe2 und 5.0-0 Be7 6.Qe2. Sergey Tiviakov himself has placed the white queen on e2 since he was six years old - 40 years of experience, he presents you with all that is important in 5 hours of video running time!

€ 29,90

Simon Williams:
THE EXCITING BUDAPEST GAMBIT

The Budapest Gambit is an exciting and entertaining way to play against 1.d4 and 2.c4 - with 1...Nf6 and 2...e5. Let the GM from England show you how you can set White unexpected problems with this fascinating opening. "On this DVD I will share my knowledge with you. Accompany me on my journey to discover the beauty and strength of the Budapest Gambit!"

€ 29,90

10...c5

Normally one of the automatic moves. But with White having played ♗a2 instead of the normal ♗c2, I am not entirely sure of this move. As we will see, the d5-square will be a juicy spot for the white pieces to sit on later in the game. Instead, I like the greedy 10...bxa4, which is what Ding played. A pawn is still a pawn, after all.

11.♗g5

A typical move in these Spanish structures. White wants to eliminate the knight in order to gain access to the d5-square.

11...0-0 12.♘bd2

12...♖b8

Tari was facing a tough decision. The move ...bxa4, which I recommended earlier, was a lot less appealing now. Still, it might have been his best choice: 12...bxa4 13.♗xf6 ♗xf6 14.♗d5 ♖a7!? (I like this odd move more than ...♖b8. It is in anticipation of what comes next) 15.♖xa4.

ANALYSIS DIAGRAM

Surely the point of Carlsen's idea. In return for the lost exchange, White acquires beautiful light-square

Magnus Carlsen provides additional advice after a positional master class. Aryan Tari had a rough time of it, but taking part in Norway Chess was an invaluable experience.

control, and the knight on a5 is left stranded. Still, after 15...♗xa4 16.♕xa4 ♕c7 I do not think Black's situation is all that bad. He can reroute his knight via d8, and at the end of the day, he has the extra material.

13.axb5 Not giving Black another chance to capture that pawn.

13...axb5 14.♖e1

14...b4? This is the first mistake of the game, and quite a whopper at that. Black gives up all the light squares on the queenside and invites the white bishop to sit pretty on d5.

15.♘c4 This is fine, but I don't

really understand what made Carlsen refrain from the simple 15.♗xf6 ♗xf6 16.♘d5, and White's position simply looks gorgeous.

15...♘xc4 16.♗xc4 bxc3 17.bxc3

17...♕c7

17...♘e8!? was an interesting possibility. The idea is to exchange Black's bad bishop on e7. And if White declines the offer, the knight finds a new home on c7: 18.♗e3 ♘c7.

18.♕c2 ♗b5?

Strategically speaking, a huge error. Not only does Black give up his only good bishop, but he also clears the

way for White's knight to c4, and eventually d5.

19.♗xb5 ♖xb5 20.♗xf6! ♗xf6 21.♘d2

Despite the reduced material, Black's position is very unpleasant. A classical good knight versus bad bishop has appeared on the board.

21...♕c6

The always resilient computer offers 21...h5!, and surprisingly it tells me that Black is not doing all that bad yet. It seems that the modern approach is to advance the flank pawns in almost any position! As far as I understand, the idea is to gain space on the kingside and create some counterplay over there.

22.♕a4 ♖fb8 23.♘c4 ♗e7

24.g3

White slowly reinforces his position, and there is not much Black can do to improve his.

24.♘a3 is an interesting option as well, forcing the queens off the board: 24...♖5b6 25.♕xc6 ♖xc6 26.♘c4. Even without queens, Black's black position looks grim. He will face a long and tough defence with no prospects here either.

24...♕c8 25.♕d1 Carlsen transfers his queen to the kingside. Slowly but surely he will start building an attack against the black king.

25...g6

25...♕h3!? would have been quite an interesting attempt, slightly disturbing White's plans by preventing ♔g2, for the moment at least.

26.♔g2 ♗f8 27.♕f3 ♖b3 28.♖ec1 ♕e6 29.♖a7 ♖8b7 30.♖xb7 ♖xb7

A set of rooks has been exchanged, but it has not improved Black's situation. The time has come for the white pieces to infiltrate the black position.

31.♖a1

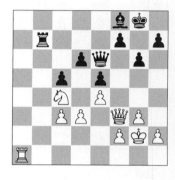

31...h5

Carlsen discussed 31...♖b3 with commentators Vladimir Kramnik and Judit Polgar during the press conference. It should not come as a surprise that Black has no time to capture pawns in this position, but the variation is instructive: 32.♘e3 ♖xc3 33.♘d5 ♖b3 34.♖a8 ♔g7 35.g4 (this is very similar to the actual game) 35...c4 36.g5 cxd3 37.♘c7 ♕e7 38.♘e8+ ♔h8 39.♘f6 ♔g7 40.♕h3 h5 41.gxh6+ ♔xf6 42.h7 ♗g7.

ANALYSIS DIAGRAM

Carlsen and the commentators got this far, assuming that this was a win for White, although they didn't actually see one. Finally Carlsen said: 'Let the computers figure it out.' And indeed, White does have a win, and a quite simple one at that: 43.♖g8!, followed by ♖xg7 and h8♕(+), wins easily.

32.♖a8 ♔g7 33.♘e3

Everything in White's position flows so smoothly. Now the knight is being transferred to the beautiful d5-square.

33...♖c7?

So far, Tari has defended quite well, but this is the decisive mistake.

Black's only chance to stop the attack was to try and exchange the rooks: 33...♕d7! (with the idea of exchanging rooks by means of ...♖a7) 34.♘d5 ♗e7!, stopping ♕f6+, and with ...♖a7 next Black's position is still tenable.

34.♘d5 ♖c8 Here the exchange of rooks is easily prevented.

35.♖a7! It goes without saying that Carlsen keeps the rooks on the board.

35...♖b8 36.h3!

The final step. The white pawns join the attack, gaining space on the

kingside and closing the net around the black king. Sadly, there is nothing Black can do to stop it.

36...♖d8 37.g4 hxg4 38.hxg4 ♖d7 39.♖a8! Once again not allowing the rook swap.

39...f6 This won't help, but there was nothing that would have.

40.g5 f5 41.♕h3! A nice switch to the h-file decides the game.

41...♖f7

42.♖e8! A pretty tactic to force resignation. **42...♕xe8 43.♕h6+ ♔g8 44.♕xg6+ ♔h8 45.♘f6** Black resigned.

∎ ∎ ∎

A daily routine in the New Normal. Chief arbiter Anemone Kulczak disinfects the pieces.

Going into Round 9, Carlsen was a point ahead of Firouzja, while Aronian – three and a half points behind – had effectively dropped out of the race. Their first game had ended in a draw from a very promising position for the World Champion, who then clinched the Armageddon game when Firouzja lost on time in a drawish position. In their second game, Firouzja seemed to be heading for another draw...

NOTES BY
Anish Giri

Alireza Firouzja
Magnus Carlsen
Stavanger 2020 (9)
Réti Opening

1.♘f3 ♘f6 2.g3 c5 3.♗g2 ♘c6

This is a pretty decent system against the Réti Opening. I believe it has gained in popularity thanks to the efforts of Sergey Karjakin, who played it exclusively for a while.

I also saw some Peter Leko games recently, and I could actually use one old idea I had played against him myself in the recent Legends tournament organized by Chess24. Magnus was obviously part of that event, too, and came booked up for this important encounter.

4.0-0 e5 5.e4 d6!? I introduced this idea to top level practice in a blitz game against Kramnik, and it has understandably become more popular. The point is that compared to the standard 5...♗e7, Black keeps the f8-bishop flexible and wants to fianchetto it to g7 instead.

6.c3!? This idea suggests itself, but my game against Leko was surprisingly the only high-level game with this move so far.

6...g6!? An attempt to stick to the same development scheme, despite White's attempt to provoke an early crisis in the centre.

6...♘xe4 7.d4 f5 is where the complications start. Peter grabbed the pawn, 8.dxe5, which is the most principled response. He was actually quite well prepared, but the variations that can arise are quite challenging, and eventually he either mixed something up or forgot and I ended up winning a miniature.

7.d4 cxd4 8.cxd4 ♗g4!

This is important – first of all fighting for the d4-square, but also connecting the a8-rook and the queen.

9.dxe5 dxe5 The position is very solid for Black, because the pawn structure is symmetrical and, depending on the neural network of your engine, White's advantage is slight, very slight or symbolic.

10.♘c3

It is also possible to try and exert pressure with moves like 10.♕b3!? or 10.♕a4!?, using the fact that White is slightly ahead in development.

10...♗g7 11.h3

White keeps playing the most obvious moves, but there are, of course, alternatives.

11...♗xf3 12.♕xd8+

Not forced either and also natural. I guess White thought that, given that he has the bishop pair, the endgame should be favourable for him. This doesn't necessarily have to be the case, though, since the d4-knight is going to be mighty strong in the endgame, too.

12...♖xd8 13.♗xf3 0-0 14.♔g2 ♘d4

Their first game ended in a draw and a curious moment when Alireza Firouzja extended his hand and Magnus Carlsen changed his mind in mid-action.

15.♗g5

White didn't have much at all, but this clearly isn't an attempt at an advantage. He could have tried to play slightly more ambitiously with, for example, 15.♖b1!?, intending ♗e3 (walking out of ...♘c2), and then finishing his development in this way. But again, the d4-knight would give Black quite decent compensation for the bishop pair, and the g7-bishop would eventually switch diagonals and activate itself via f8.

15...h6 16.♗xf6 ♗xf6 17.♘d5 ♖d6 The position is now almost completely symmetrical. Black gives up the c-file, but White has little to gain from this. At this point, I saw Magnus going into the confession booth, where he said that after ...♗d8, followed by ...f7-f5, only he would be able to boast a slight edge, and that, although this does look quite elegant, objectively White doesn't have any issues with equalizing just yet.

18.♖ac1 ♗d8

19.♖fd1 White is slowly but surely losing the thread.

19.♖c8 ♔g7 (19...f5 is not a big deal. After, for example, 20.♖d1 Black doesn't actually have a threat) 20.♖fc1 would be much more natural, keeping firm control of the c-file, if only to ensure that Black won't take hold of it.

19...♔g7 20.♘e3?!

The best square for the knight was d5, and as I already pointed out, ...f7-f5 would pack no threats.

20...♖a6 21.a3 h5 22.♘c4?!

Misplacing the knight.

22...♗f6 23.h4?! ♖c8!

It is quite ironic. White was uncomfortable when he controlled the c-file himself, and now he is equally uncomfortable with the file in his opponent's control

Black seizes the opportunity to grab the c-file – for what it's worth!

24.♘e3

24.♖xd4 is spectacular, but after 24...exd4 25.e5 ♖c7! the tactic backfires, since the c4-knight is pinned and ...b5 is coming.

24...♖ac6 25.♖xc6 ♖xc6 26.♖d3 Now White does the same and neutralizes the c-file with ♗d1.

26...♗d8 27.♗d1 ♖c1 28.♗b3 b5

Black is trying to exert as much pressure as he can, but his resources are rather limited.

29.♖d1 ♖c8 30.♗a2 a5

31.♖d3?!

A very panicky attempt to try and trade rooks.

31.♗b1! was simple and strong, just transferring the bishop to d3, where it controls all entry squares. With the knight returning to d5, there is little to worry about here. It is quite ironic. White was uncomfortable

when he controlled the c-file himself, and now he is equally uncomfortable with the file in his opponent's control – a distilled demonstration of the psychology of top-level chess these days.

31...a4!

As we will see in the game, ♖c3 will now be met with takes and ...♘b3!.

32.♔f1 ♗b6 33.♖c3?

Pursuing the bad plan. Now White will get into serious trouble.

33...♖xc3 34.bxc3 ♘b3!

The knight is very annoying here.

35.♔e1 ♗c5 36.♘c2

The best position Black has had in this game. White doesn't really have a way to extricate himself, his bishop is blinded by the b3-knight and the c2-knight is tied to the defence of the a3-pawn. The king is committed to the kingside pawns (and has nowhere to go anyway). Everything is perfect for Black, but now he decides to force matters, miscalculating on the way.

36...♘c1?

36...f5! would have maintained the pressure. The position would also be a lot easier to play for Black than for White. A big miss. 37.exf5 gxf5, and it is hard to suggest a move for White. I guess just sit and wait, while Black improves his position and in the end possibly still goes for ...♘c1-d3, albeit in a better version.

37.♗d5 ♘d3+ 38.♔e2 ♘xf2 39.♗c6 Here it probably occurred to Magnus that ♘e3! was coming. White is escaping.

39...f6

39...f5 won't do Black any good either after 40.exf5 gxf5 41.♘e3!.

40.♞e3! ♞h1
Black is still trying, but the queen-side pawns are going to cancel each other out, and there are just too few resources left on the kingside, since the knight is semi-trapped on h1.
41.♞f1! ♝xa3 42.♝xb5 ♝b2 43.♝xa4 ♝xc3 44.♔f3

With Black's knight on a decent square, he would probably have been able to exert more pressure, but in order to try and bring it back into the game, he would have to allow two more pawn trades with g4 and h5.
44...♝d4 45.g4 hxg4+ 46.♔xg4 ♞f2+ 47.♔f3 ♔h6 48.♞g3 ♞d3 49.♝e8 ♞f4 50.♞e2 ♞e6 51.♝f7 ♞c5 52.♞g3

Now h4-h5 is inevitable, and Magnus

On the free day the players were treated to another culinary competition. Levon Aronian's cake won.

asks the final mini-question.
52...♝c3 53.h5

53...♝e1!?
Going for a good knight vs bad bishop ending, but there are just too few pawns here.
53...gxh5 54.♞xh5 is utterly drawn. The opposite-coloured bishops and the lack of pawns make it all too easy for White to hold this.
54.♝xg6 ♝xg3 55.♔xg3 ♔g5
The h5-pawn is doomed, but White doesn't need it to secure the draw.
56.♔f3 ♞b3 57.♝f7 ♞d4+

58.♔g3 ♞e2+ 59.♔f3 ♞f4 60.♔g3 ♞xh5+

61.♝xh5
The pawn ending is a trivial draw, but the position actually even holds if White allows his king to be pushed back, e.g. 61.♔f3 ♔h4 62.♝e6 ♞f4 63.♝c8 ♞h3 64.♔f5 ♞g5+, and now the easiest way is to just play ♔f2. As it turns out, the position is objectively a draw, even if White makes further concessions after 65.♔e3 ♔g3 66.♔d2 ♔f4 67.♔d3.

ANALYSIS DIAGRAM

Here one could imagine a scenario in which Black would win (e.g. check on f2 or c5), but in reality White can hold there, too, if he shifts his king from d3 to d5 at the right time.
61...♔xh5 62.♔h3 ♔h6 63.♔h4
Immediately going for the distant opposition with 63.♔h2 is kind of prettier. I once had a similar endgame with colours reversed, and I remember I was very impressed when my opponent played ...♔g7-h8! with my king on h2 and pawns on g4, h4 and h6.
63...♔g7 64.♔g3 ♔f8 65.♔f2 ♔e7

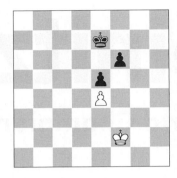

66.♔e2?! This will also hold (apparently there is a rule that it doesn't matter if there are pawns between the kings), but it shows that White doesn't really get the concept.
66.♔e3! is more to the point, keeping the kings separated by an odd number of squares.
66...♔e8 67.♔e3 ♔d7 68.♔d3
Somehow 68.♔d2!? ♔d6 69.♔d3 is a dual because of the fact that ...♔d5 is impossible in that position, but again, the draw is automatic once you know the concept of distant opposition.
68...♔d6

69.♔c3?? I am sure that with more time on the clock White would have figured it out, but with only seconds, the somewhat counterintuitive (White is trying to prevent the black king from advancing and takes a step back instead of blocking it at once) concept of the distant opposition turned out to be too hard to find.
Correct was 69.♔d2! – obviously – maintaining that distant opposition.
69...♔c5 0-1. GGYO, as a God of Chess, Hikaru Nakamura likes to say.

Time for bullet
This win sealed Carlsen's third Norway Chess win with one round to spare. In the press conference he suggested that he might be satisfied with a simple draw in his last game against Aronian. Whether he still harboured that wish when he sat down for that final game is unclear. His play was dithering and soon Black was playing for a win and won.

Another failed attempt to shake hands after their second game. In severe time-trouble Alireza Firouzja totally lost control, handing Magnus Carlsen the 3 points that secured first place.

After resigning Carlsen fled the playing room, avoiding a final press conference. Later he posted a reaction on Twitter: 'Lost deservedly in the last round of Norway Chess today, which luckily did not matter in terms of tournament standings. There certainly were some positive moments, but mostly I felt pretty clueless throughout the tournament. Even long thinks generally resulted in guesses. Nevertheless, happy to be playing over the board and classical again, and a huge thanks to the organizer for making it possible and safe for us. Don't know when I'll be playing a classical tournament again, but I'll be eagerly awaiting the opportunity, and try to improve.'

Later that night, or rather in the middle of the night, at 1 am, the World Champion resurfaced on Lichess, where he embarked on a bullet match against Andrew Tang. The match against the American GM – and bullet specialist – lasted two hours and 10 minutes, and 79(!) games. The score: 48-31 in Carlsen's favour. He was winning again. ∎

Stavanger 2020			1	2	3	4	5	6	TOTAL	TPR
1 Magnus Carlsen	NOR	2863	* *	1½ 3	1½ 0	3 1½	0 3	3 3	19½	2845
2 Alireza Firouzja	FIDE	2728	1 0	* *	1½ 1½	1½ 1	3 3	3 3	18½	2872
3 Levon Aronian	ARM	2767	1 3	1 1	* *	3 0	3 1	3 1½	17½	2864
4 Fabiano Caruana	USA	2828	0 1	1 1½	0 3	* *	3 1½	3 1½	15½	2778
5 Jan-Krzysztof Duda	POL	2757	3 0	0 0	0 1½	0 1	* *	1 3	9½	2652
6 Aryan Tari	NOR	2633	0 0	0 0	0 1	0 1	1½ 0	* *	3½	2497

3 points for a win, 1½ for Armageddon win, 1 for Armageddon loss

William Steinitz

A fresh look at a misunderstood World Champion

For many years William Steinitz was the strongest chess master in the world and in 1886 he became the first official World Champion when he defeated his rival Zukertort 12½-7½ in a match played in New York, St. Louis and New Orleans. **TIM HARDING**, whose book *Steinitz in London* has just been published by McFarland, explains why Steinitz deserves a reassessment.

Steinitz's early attacking style led some to call him 'the Austrian Morphy'. Undoubtedly, he studied Morphy's games closely, but his mature style became very different.

S teinitz, the first World Chess Champion, might seem to today's young players to be a remote figure, but to dismiss him as irrelevant would be a big mistake. A man must be judged by the times he lived in, and any chess master by the knowledge and standards of his day. Steinitz, who won the title after a match victory over his rival Zukertort in 1886, was a pioneer in many respects, and was rightly honoured when FIDE named the first big online blitz tournament in May of this year the Steinitz Memorial.

The idea of a blitz tournament would have been alien to Steinitz because the chess clocks of his day (first introduced in 1883) were too delicate for the hurly-burly of five-minute chess. Fast 'skittles' play (without clocks) was certainly not unknown to his contemporaries such as Henry Bird, but Steinitz liked time to think. The rate of play in tournaments of his day, though slower than elite events nowadays, was often too fast for his liking; consequently he made a poor start to competitions until he adjusted. In match play, where he could insist on four minutes or more per move, Steinitz was invincible for more than a quarter of a century – except when he tried to give the young Cecil De Vere odds of pawn and move in 1865.

Steinitz was born in Prague in 1836, to a humble Jewish family. His original given name was Wolf but he preferred Wilhelm, which was gradually Anglicised to William during the 1860s. In his childhood years, Prague was a provincial capital in the Austrian empire and had little chess tradition. There is no record of his returning there in later years. Yet, Steinitz must have become a fairly proficient player before, at the age of 22, he moved to Vienna to study at its Polytechnic.

Steinitz's early chess career developed in the shadow of Paul Morphy, the American genius who won the first American Chess

In match play, where he could insist on four minutes or more per move, he was invincible for more than a quarter of a century

Congress of 1857 and conquered everyone whom he met on his European tour of 1858/9 before retiring from chess almost completely. Steinitz's early attacking style of play led some to call him 'the Austrian Morphy' and indeed Steinitz had undoubtedly studied Morphy's games closely, although his mature style became very different. When in 1882 he first visited the USA and spent some time in New Orleans, he made sure to meet Morphy. Then when Steinitz began his *International Chess Magazine* in 1885, his first major article was an assessment of Morphy's play. Steinitz's magazine went through

seven volumes, concluding in early 1892, and collectors treasure the handsome bound volumes. (The less fortunate of us can be satisfied with the reprints produced by Olms or Moravian Chess.) Evidently Steinitz liked fine chess literature and his book of the 1889 New York Chess Congress (of which he was principal organiser) is another collector's item.

Steinitz's earliest known games date from 1859. In May 1862, after winning the Vienna club's annual tournament at his fourth attempt (not the third, as usually stated), he travelled to the British capital to compete at the London 1862 congress. To provide an illustration of his play on the eve of his departure, here is a game that until recently was unknown.

Dr. Friedrich Nowotny
William Steinitz
Vienna Chess Club Championship
1861/1862
1.e4 e5 2.♘f3 ♘c6 3.♗c4 ♗c5 4.0-0 d6 5.c3 ♘f6 6.d4 exd4 7.cxd4 ♗b6 8.♘c3 ♗g4 9.♗b5 0-0 10.♗xc6 bxc6 11.♗g5 h6 12.♗h4 g5 13.♗g3 ♗xf3 14.gxf3

Group portrait, probably taken on July 5th 1873. Sitting: William Steinitz, chess patron H. F. Gastineau and Cecil De Vere. Standing: J. Lovelock, B. Horwitz, W. N. Potter, J. J. Löwenthal, H. F. Down, J. H. Blackburne and Dr. W. Ballard.

♘h5 15.♔h1 ♕f6 16.e5 ♘xg3+ 17.fxg3 dxe5 18.dxe5 ♕xe5 19.f4 ♕g7 20.fxg5 hxg5 21.♕d7 ♖ad8 22.♕xc6 ♖d6 23.♕f3 ♖h6 24.♘d5 f6 25.g4 ♕h7 26.♕e2 ♖f7 27.♖ad1?

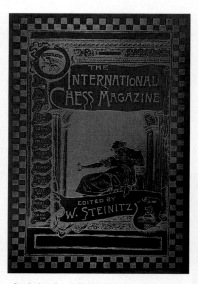

27...♖xh2+ 28.♕xh2 ♕e4+ 29.♕g2 ♖h7 Mate.

The style of play which served to defeat Austrian amateurs was too unsophisticated to succeed against some of the seasoned masters Steinitz met in London, but he did well enough to make a strong impression on the President of the London Chess Club, Augustus Mongredien. The club sponsored a match with the Italian master Dubois which Steinitz won. Thereafter he remained

in England for over twenty years although for much of that time his financial situation was precarious. He won good prize money in some years, but the life of a chess professional has rarely meant prosperity.

Steinitz set new standards in chess journalism through the chess column which he conducted in *The Field*

Census records, which reveal the occupations of other people living in the houses that Steinitz and his family shared in 1871 and 1881, prove the truth of what he once told the Scottish-Canadian economist James Mavor: 'Here am I,' he said, 'the most successful chess professional of my time, winner of the most important prizes in chess matches and editor of the most important and remunerative chess column, and yet, on the average, I have not received more than the wages of an artisan.'

A shilling a game

Tournaments were few and far between, and as a foreigner Steinitz was ineligible to compete in some of

them. Therefore much of his chess in those years was played in cafés for a stake of one shilling a game (equivalent to about 5 pounds, 6 euros or 7 US dollars today) and sometimes giving odds of a knight or even a rook. Steinitz's first big opportunity came when a wealthy patron backed him to challenge German master Adolf Anderssen, winner of the 1851 and 1862 London tournaments, to a match for £100 a side, the equivalent of more than 10,000 euro in today's money. Before play began on 18 July 1866, Steinitz prepared carefully, studying a book of Anderssen's games which Gustav Neumann had recently published. The fight was tense, but Anderssen undoubtedly made his task more difficult by avoiding draws in some of the games. At the critical moment when the score stood at 6-6, Steinitz raised the level of his play another notch. He took the 13th and 14th games to win the stakes and show that he was one of the top players in Europe. In later years he would date his tenure of the World Championship to this victory, but there was no official title for another twenty years.

Steinitz also set new standards in chess journalism through the chess column which he conducted in *The Field* from late 1873 until July 1882. His annotations were deeper than those of previous writers and he reported on major events in detail. London was then the centre of the chess world; from 1878 to 1882 four of the world's top six players lived there.

In October 1882, after resigning from *The Field* following his Vienna victory, Steinitz began an exploratory tour of America. He returned for the London 1883 tournament, but

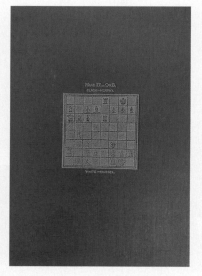

Steinitz for bibliophiles. The decoratively bound volumes of *The International Chess Magazine* are sought after by collectors. A gold-coloured diagram of Morphy's queen sacrifice against Paulsen in the First American Congress of 1857 graced the cover of *The Modern Chess Instructor* (1889).

thereafter settled permanently in New York. He became a naturalized United States citizen in 1888, two years after earning the world title by his second match victory over Zukertort. Steinitz defended the world crown successfully in three matches (two against Chigorin and one against Gunsberg) until poor health and Emanuel Lasker, leader of a new generation of opponents, caught up with him in 1894. Steinitz never returned to Europe until 1895. Financial necessity obliged him to make four tours to the old continent in his final years because it offered greater opportunities of earning money from chess.

A good Austrian

Of the major cities in his life, Steinitz perhaps liked Vienna best. Although he only lived there from (approximately) August 1858 until April 1862, all his life he had Viennese friends. At the dinner after the 1873 international tournament, which he had just concluded with a 16-game winning streak, Steinitz made a lengthy speech to please his hosts and said he always considered himself a good Austrian. This did not prevent him leading the London team against Vienna in the correspondence match of 1872/74. In 1882 Steinitz won at Vienna again and it was there that he went once more to recuperate in the spring of 1897 after the mental breakdown in Moscow which followed his abject failure to regain the world title from Lasker.

Steinitz had also made a detour to Vienna before that match. In October 1896, he had been preparing at the Bavarian spa of Bad Wörishofen. It would have been more direct to travel to Russia via Berlin, but he chose to renew his American passport in Vienna, probably because the chess master Max Judd was U.S. consul there. Steinitz's final visit to Vienna was for the marathon 1898 tournament in which he very creditably won fourth prize. Only a few of the 19 contestants had the

energy to go on straight to Cologne for another tournament, but Steinitz, though now 62 years old, came fifth there. The following year, however, he was visibly diminished at the London 1899 international and for the only time in his life finished outside the prize list. That was the end of his career and he died in New York in August 1900.

Filling a gap

There is as yet no fully reliable biography of the champion because the well-known work by the late Kurt Landsberger (*William Steinitz, Chess Champion*, McFarland 1993) although well-researched for Steinitz's final years, does not cover his English period satisfactorily. *Steinitz in London* develops in much more detail the chapter about him in my earlier book *Eminent Victorian Chess Players* (McFarland 2012). It deals chiefly with the years 1862 to 1882 when Steinitz's game developed to maturity and when his biggest personal battles were fought. My Steinitz database currently has about 1200 games, of which roughly half are in the book; it does not include games played in America or in Europe of the 1890s, which I leave as a task for some future biographer. *Steinitz in London* also includes a broad portrait of the London chess scene in the nineteenth century, with sections on the history of the city's main chess clubs and the famous Simpson's Divan where Steinitz spent so much of his time.

How strong was he really?

It is hard to judge from Steinitz's games how strong a player he was. In his day there were few other professionals or amateurs who played consistently at master level. The harsh verdict of computers on old champions is anachronistic because the general level of opening theory, positional understanding and especially defensive technique has progressed so much in the past century. American sprinter Jesse

Wilhelm Steinitz

1836	Born in Prague, then capital of the Austrian province of Bohemia.
1858	Moves to Vienna, enrolling as a student at the Polytechnic.
1862	Wins the Vienna Chess Club tournament, then moves to London, winning 6th prize in the international chess tournament.
1866	Defeats Adolf Anderssen in a 14-game match.
1873	Wins the Vienna international tournament and becomes chess editor of *The Field*.
1876	Defeats Joseph Blackburne 7-0 in a match before retiring from competitive play. Becomes chess editor of the *London Figaro*.
1882	Resumes competition, winning at Vienna again, but both his chess columns end. Begins a tour of the USA in November.
1883	Emigrates to America after finishing second to Johannes Zukertort in London tournament.
1885	Publication of the *International Chess Magazine* commences.
1886	Defeats Zukertort in first official World Championship match.
1889	Defends the world title in a match against Mikhail Chigorin. Organises the 6th American Chess Congress in New York; edits the congress book.
1894	Loses the world title to Emanuel Lasker.
1895	Plays in Hastings and resumes participation in European competitions.
1900	August 12. Dies in New York.

Owens set a world record of 10.2 seconds for 100 metres in 1936 which stood for twenty years; we would not say now that he was a slow runner even though that time would no longer be sufficient to qualify for the Olympic Games. Rather we would believe that if Owens were a young

A broadside announcing the Steinitz-Zukertort World Championship match. After four hours the games were interrupted for dinner and continued in the evening.

man today, using modern training methods, he would still be one of the best. That is how we should regard the top chess players of the past.

Gradually Steinitz developed from being a talented but raw tactician to the strongest player the world had yet seen. During his twenty years in London he developed positional concepts and learned to take fewer risks. Writing after the London 1883 tournament, where he finished second to Zukertort, William Norwood Potter, who knew both masters well, wrote (in his chess column for *Land and Water*) the following

the same as it was with Steinitz, who came over here in 1862, expecting to do grand things, but who, in the congress of that year, received a salutary lesson, for he then only took sixth prize, whereas four years afterwards he was able to defeat the then world's champion, Anderssen.'

A paradox about Steinitz is that, time and again, he failed to align his opening repertoire with his new strategic ideas, returning to dubious variations that had served him well in his early career. Incompletely developed positional theories led him dogmatically to persist with experiments such as

not the superior of Blackburne and Zukertort. His inferiority to Chigorin in that respect was clearly shown in their telegraph match of 1890/91. Steinitz was, though, a terrific fighter at the board.

Professor Arpad Elo, in his pioneering book *The Rating of Chessplayers Past and Present*, calculated a sustained peak rating of 2650 for Steinitz. Two modern statisticians offer comparative calculations for historic players. The *chessmetrics* website of Jeff Sonas estimates a peak three-year rating for Steinitz of 2794 based on the years 1884-1886, but in those years, except for his World Championship match against Zukertort (where he lost some early games), Steinitz was just crushing American amateurs. I have more faith in the methodology and historical research underlying the Edo ratings calculated by Professor Rod Edwards at www.edochess.ca. His estimate of Steinitz's strength in those years is close to Elo's but the Canadian mathematician more credibly reckons his peak to have been between the years 1872 and 1876, when Steinitz won two master tournaments and trounced both his main London rivals in matches. Edwards has Steinitz at 2778 in 1872, 2773 in 1873 and reaching his top rating of 2784 in 1876.

Full of errors

Another issue complicating the assessment of Steinitz's play is that the databases and books where his games can be found are full of errors. Several game scores, even from some of his World Championship matches, are often given incorrectly.

Particularly problematic is the sixth game of the 1866 Anderssen match in London.

William Steinitz
Adolf Anderssen
London 1866, 6th match game
1.e4 c5 2.g3 ♘c6 3.♗g2 e5 4.♘e2 ♘f6 5.♘bc3 d6 6.0-0 ♗e7 7.f4 h5 8.h3 ♗d7 9.♘d5 ♕c8

Gradually Steinitz developed from being a talented but raw tactician to the strongest player the world had yet seen

astute analysis of their development: 'Zukertort... like Steinitz... had to go through a course of what we will call the English style of play, which aims at methodic calculation, soundness of combination, and a severe accuracy. The result of a union between German genius and British self-mastery has been with Zukertort

2.e5 against the French Defence and some of his more outlandish defences to the Evans Gambit. His desire to test his ideas often jeopardised the scoring of tournament points. Steinitz was vulnerable defending tactical positions where material was sacrificed for the initiative, and as an analyst of complicated tactics he was

**10.♘xf6+ ♝xf6 11.f5 ♘e7 12.c4
♕d8 13.♘c3 ♝c6 14.d3 ♕d7
15.a3 a5 16.b3 b5**

At this point both contemporary and modern sources differ on what was played. Following *The Chess Player's Magazine*, most books and databases have **17.♝e3** but the first published score (from Staunton's column in the *Illustrated London News*) shows 17.♝d2 instead. Since Staunton was involved in the match organisation, there is good reason to suppose he had the authentic version. Current databases say the game continued **17...b4 18.axb4 cxb4 19.♘a4 ♝xa4 20.♖xa4 ♘c6 21.♕d2 ♝d8 22.d4 ♝b6 23.d5 ♕a7 24.♝xb6 ♕xb6+ 25.♔h1 ♘d8 26.♕g5 ♔f8 27.f6 g6 28.h4 ♘b7** In Staunton's version White's dark-squared bishop took two moves to reach e3 and Black in the meantime had moved his queen's rook to c8. There followed 30.♝h3 ♖d8 in Staunton's version but databases have **29.♝h3 ♖d8** Now the same position has arisen in each case.

When Grandmaster Robert Hübner analysed this game in an article

Steinitz in 1897, when he suffered a mental breakdown after his abject failure to regain the world title from Lasker.

about the match for *Schachkalender 2016*, he rightly called Black's 29...♖d8 a 'completely incomprehensible move' (*ein völlig unverständlicher Zug*). As several writers had pointed out before him, Black could instead have played 29...♘c5, attacking both a4 and b3. This wins decisive material, because if 30.♝f5 ♘xa4 31.bxa4 b3 32.♝xg6 ♕c7 White cannot break through on the kingside (Hübner). On the other hand, in Staunton's version White's move ♝h3 attacks the black rook which is on c8, which is another strong reason for believing that 17.♝d2 was actually played.

My book indicates numerous discrepancies between versions of Steinitz games. Many of these were detected using a suite of chess software developed by Thomas Niessen of Aachen (see https://thomastonk.jimdofree.com). Niessen has previously pointed out that the scores of about 14 per cent of the games played in the Hastings 1895 tournament differ between the official

English language tournament book, edited by Horace Cheshire, and Emil Schallopp's German-language book, which is often the more reliable. Perhaps the most serious case is the finish of the game Lasker-Steinitz.

Lasker-Steinitz
Hastings 1895
position after 37.♖d1

The game actually concluded **37...♕f7 38.♝c4 ♝e6 39.e5 ♝xc4 40.♘f5 1-0.** Cheshire printed Black's 37th move as 'Q to B sq.' (i.e., 37...♕c8) with White's 38th move giving check, but if the black queen were really on c8, White's 40th move, instead of being decisive, would just put the knight *en prise*. That 37...♕f7 is correct can be verified from the London *Daily News* of 17 August 1895 and the *Deutsche Schachzeitung* for September 1895.

Precarious state of health

Another complication in assessing Steinitz's playing strength is that between 1873 and 1882 he played no competitive chess at all except for the match with Blackburne in February 1876 which he won 7-0. The reason for Steinitz's temporary retirement was twofold. Firstly, there was the financial security that his literary work provided him, counterbalanced by the time required each week to write his articles for *The Field* and (from August 1876) the *London Figaro*. Secondly, there was his precarious state of health, about which he often complained. In a letter dated April 27th 1876 to the German master Von der Lasa (which was quoted in an article by Landsberger for *Quarterly for Chess History*), Steinitz wrote 'I am very short-sighted, my eyes are very weak.' Other sources also testify to problems with his eyes and his legs, but it is likely he was exaggerating for effect when he wrote in the same letter that he possessed 'on the whole very little theoretical knowledge' and did not have a strong memory. His correspondent, after all, was the editor of the major treatise, the *Handbuch des Schachspiels*, and this letter was written at a time when Steinitz appears to have been undergoing some kind of mental crisis.

Steinitz, according to his contemporaries, spoke English with a strong accent (saying 'beer-shops' for bishops, for example), but he was able to write the language fluently and with some style. In 1877, after 15 years' residence in Britain, Steinitz would have been eligible to apply for

The cartoon in *The Westminster Papers* that portrayed Steinitz as a short-sighted dwarf hunched over a chessboard.

British citizenship, as the Hungarian-born Löwenthal had done before him in 1866. Löwenthal, it was said,

could pass for an English country gentleman but Steinitz never wanted to be British. He became increasingly embittered and in 1886 wrote that he would rather die in America than live in England.

An argumentative personality

Some of the more colourful episodes in Steinitz's career arose from his argumentative personality and strong principles, which led him to be involved in several public disputes. He would rarely back down even when it would have been pragmatic to do so. Although prejudice against foreigners, especially Jews, may have been less pronounced in London chess circles than in middle-class society in general, the prevalent cult of the amateur in sport weighed heavily against him.

Staunton, though no longer an active player, wielded immense influence through his chess column

SOURCE: CHESS IN ART

A colourful painting of the first official world title match between Zukertort and Steinitz in 1886 by American artist Charles Henry Granger (1812-1893).

and was quite hypocritical in his views about playing chess for money, one of his contemporaries remembering 'I knew him when he was glad to play for threepence a game.' The two crossed swords, metaphorically speaking, at the end of 1866, when both were members of the new Westminster Chess Club. Steinitz 'in private conversation expressed myself in the strongest terms about his (Staunton's) conduct against Morphy.' This was a reference to Staunton's avoidance in 1858 of a match against Morphy which was exacerbated by some misleading statements Staunton made about the American in his *Illustrated London News* chess column. Also in late 1866, Steinitz's match with Bird had come to an end prematurely because the latter was called to America on urgent business. Steinitz insisted on claiming the stakes rather than accept an indefinite postponement and for this he was widely vilified.

It motivated Staunton, already irked by the Anderssen result, to write a libellous article in which he denounced professionalism in chess. When Steinitz sought a retraction, Staunton tried to use his 'clout' to have Steinitz expelled from the Westminster Club. That failed, but a false friend (whom Steinitz never named) tricked him into resigning from the society, from which Staunton himself was obliged to depart a few months later.

In 1875 Steinitz alienated himself from a larger circle of British chess amateurs. He unwisely took a leading part in the founding of a chess club in the West End of London as a breakaway from the City of London Chess Club where he was a committee member. The ensuing controversy led to Steinitz and other professionals resigning from the latter club, and he made matters worse at the same time by writing a vindictive review of an openings book by the popular R. B. Wormald.

The chess magazine *Westminster Papers*, in its March 1876 issue, published a satirical cartoon (see the previous page) portraying Steinitz as a short-sighted dwarf hunched over a chessboard. The accompanying text referred to his 'conscientious attachment to his own interest in every transaction of his public life' and said that he had 'rather neglected most of the branches of polite learning which are said to lend a charm to social intercourse'.

What Steinitz later referred to as the 'sanguine battles in the campaign under the board' came to a head in 1877 after a row at the Divan which led him to be excluded for several weeks. Prominent chess journalists led by Patrick Thomas Duffy published a series of articles attacking Steinitz's mercenary characteristics, calling him a 'shilling hunter'. When Zukertort, in a letter to one of the papers, took Steinitz's side, Duffy in reply rejoiced that the West End Club had just closed, calling it 'the happy hunting-ground of the noisiest German band in London, the gentry who believe that it is highly "creditable" to "win" other people's money. Among Englishmen there is a strong preference for *earning* it.' Steinitz's replies mostly hinged on his correct assertion that it was disgraceful that so many chess columns were in the hands of Duffy, who had no track record as a player and was a poor judge of a chess problem.

In his final London years Steinitz gravitated to the elite St. George's Club, where he had some strong supporters including the club secretary James Innes Minchin. Yet Steinitz eventually found enemies there too and resigned his honorary membership following disputes at the London 1883 tournament.

The Ink War

Steinitz's last and bitterest war in print was with Leopold Hoffer, co-editor with Zukertort of *The Chess-Monthly* since its commencement in 1879.

In the next issue of his magazine Steinitz responded with a verse of his own where Hoffer was called a rat with 'lunatic eyes'

Steinitz had assisted Hoffer when he came to London in 1870 as a refugee from the Franco-Prussian War, but little gratitude was evident. In the January 1882 number of that magazine came the first salvos in what chess historian Ken Whyld called the 'Ink War'. It began with seemingly trivial disagreements over rival analyses of games in the 1881 Blackburne versus Zukertort match, but Hoffer made it personal when he wrote: 'We cannot, therefore, join the proposed *mutual admiration society*, in which a Chess Editor would stand, like a Stylites of old, on his column sacrosanct, and calling anathema at the slightest sign of doubt in his infallibility.'

The rights and wrongs of the analyses are irrelevant but these early arguments, together with renewed rivalry between Steinitz and Zukertort when the former returned to active play, festered alongside negotiations for the match between them which took four years to arrange. Steinitz came to believe that Hoffer had stolen his *Field* column, although the exact course of events which led to Steinitz resigning the post and losing his regular income do not support conspiracy theories. When Steinitz started his own magazine, he had a new platform to strike back. In the December 1888 number of *International Chess Magazine*, Steinitz first introduced the abusive term Dreckseele ('Filth-Soul') to address Hoffer; he claimed that this epithet had been coined by Bernhard Horwitz. In reply Hoffer referred to Steinitz as 'Quasimodo'.

Their exchanges of insults became most vicious in May 1889 when *The Chess-Monthly* published a curious piece of verse entitled 'Nits will be Lice', which ended 'who with barge-pole, boots or tongs would touch Bohemian sty-nits?' In the next issue

of his magazine Steinitz responded with a verse of his own where Hoffer was called a rat with 'lunatic eyes'. *The Chess-Monthly* went too far in its September issue which included far more defamatory material about Steinitz. The 30 stanzas of 'Song of a Nit' abused not only him but his partner also. Hoffer had to print a new section to replace the offending pages in bound volumes.

Let us not conclude on that sour note but instead admire one of Steinitz's best games. On occasion he could revert to the brilliance of his youth, as his attack against Von Bardeleben at Hastings 1895 showed, but that game is well known and not typical. The following victory has long been recognised (by Lasker and Kasparov among others) as one of the best examples of Steinitz's mature style. Except for one lapse which was not exploited, he frustrated his opponent's attempts to make combinations until Black's position was so overwhelming that tactics worked in his favour.

Johannes Zukertort
William Steinitz
St. Louis 1886, 9th match game
1.d4 d5 2.c4 e6 3.♘c3 ♘f6 4.♘f3 dxc4 5.e3 c5 6.♗xc4 cxd4 7.exd4 ♗e7 8.0-0 0-0 9.♕e2 ♘bd7 10.♗b3 ♘b6 11.♗f4 ♘bd5 12.♗g3 ♕a5 13.♖ac1 ♗d7 14.♘e5 ♖fd8 15.♕f3 ♗e8 16.♖fe1 It must be noted that both Kasparov's book and Neishtadt's Russian work *Pyervy Chempyon Mira* have the wrong move order here. **16...♖ac8 17.♗h4 ♘xc3 18.bxc3 ♕c7 19.♕d3 ♘d5 20.♗xe7 ♕xe7 21.♗xd5?!** Zukertort, wanting to initiate a kingside attack with the rook lift that follows, prematurely exchanges Black's knight. Steinitz's own annotations passed over this strategic error in silence; Lasker was

the first to criticise it. **21...♖xd5 22.c4 ♖dd8 23.♖e3 ♕d6 24.♖d1 f6 25.♖h3 h6! 26.♘g4 ♕f4! 27.♘e3 ♗a4 28.♖f3 ♕d6 29.♖d2**

29...♗c6?!
Steinitz thought this was a good move, and Lasker did not comment, but the Yugoslav analyst V. Vukovic indicated 29...b5!, which would break White's structure.
30.♖g3?
Zukertort misses his last opportunity to create complications by 30.d5, with perhaps roughly equal chances. Each new generation of computer engines comes to a different conclusion about this difficult position which would make an excellent training exercise.
30...f5 31.♖g6 ♗e4 32.♕b3 ♔h7!

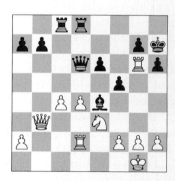

Steinitz is now ready to refute Zukertort's final attempt at combination. **33.c5 ♖xc5 34.♖xe6 ♖c1+ 35.♘d1 ♕f4 36.♕b2 ♖b1 37.♕c3 ♖c8! 38.♖xe4 ♕xe4 0-1** ∎

Tim Harding: *Steinitz in London, A Chess Biography with 623 Games*. Library binding, 421 pages, McFarland 2020

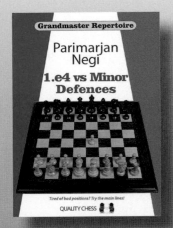

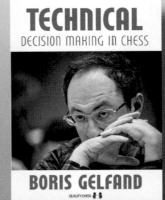

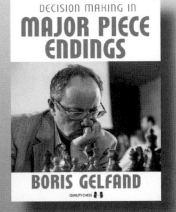
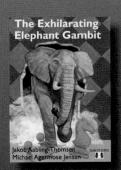
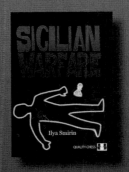

Nostalgic for the real *Saint Louis*

So and Carlsen share first prize in online Rapid & Blitz

In the face of the pandemic, the Saint Louis Chess Club had no choice but to cancel activities and move flagship events like the annual Rapid & Blitz online. The Rapid saw Wesley So sensationally take the lead ahead of Magnus Carlsen, who suffered an annoying disconnect. In the Blitz, the World Champion fought back to share the spoils with the quiet American. **ALEJANDRO RAMIREZ** saw lots of excitement, but couldn't help missing 'the real thing'.

Commentators are always supposed to be unbiased, not only towards the players, but also towards the tournaments that invite us. But, much like rooting for your favourite player during broadcast is hard to avoid, having a special place in your heart for one event over the others comes quite naturally. For me that has always been the Saint Louis Rapid and Blitz and Sinquefield Cup combination. Some great tournament memories happened at these events. Things like David Navara coming to the Spanish commentary booth, apologizing for his bad Spanish, and then giving a 15 minute monologue on his games in fluent Spanish. Playing bughouse with Levon Aronian and Yasser Seirawan, the infamous Lawrence Trent-Magnus Carlsen rook odds match... The club usually pays me to commentate this event every year, but if they didn't I would still be there every day.

For months the Saint Louis Chess Club clung to the hope of organizing its flagship events in person later this year. As the Covid-19 situation in America kept getting worse and worse, the clear disappointment sunk in that the Sinquefield Cup had to be cancelled and that the Rapid & Blitz would have to be held online. Not being able to go in person this time was a bit depressing, not being involved in the commentary was truly sad.

Inevitably, the tournament simply wasn't the same, but, as with much of the year, we do the best we can. As a spectator, the novelty of all these online events has completely faded. This year's online 'Olympiad' was anything but a success. The cheating allegations on everything from the PRO chess league to the U.S. High School Championships evidenced that there is no way around these problems for the majority of tournaments.

Great choices

The top players had already complained in previous years that they would like to see some variety in the players that they faced in the Saint Louis Rapid & Blitz. However, inviting players outside of the elite can be dangerous. This year's invitees outside of the top-10 were Pentala Harikrishna, Jeffery Xiong and Alireza Firouzja, which I thought were simply great choices.

The format of the event was unchanged from the formula of previous years: nine rounds of rapid over three days, followed by eighteen blitz games over two; rapids counting for double the points. The platform was lichess.org, which seems to be the go-to platform for the club. Like with most tournaments that are held online, the organizers must do a bit of prayer to the internet gods so that the event runs smoothly. Those gods had other plans, even from day one.

After the debacle of disconnections during the 'Olympiad', many fingers were pointed at chess.com and FIDE for not having a contingency back-up for this problem. Some even mentioned that they should learn from e-sports and see how they solve these problems. For me, as an avid fan of e-sports and someone that worked for a major e-sports company, the solution to the disconnection problem has always been simple: high paying tournaments are played on LAN (local area networks) so as not to have to deal with this.

Online events are riddled with lag and disconnections and problems. It's part of the internet, and it affects the chess world even worse than most e-sports. Even though it is a turn-based game, we don't have a pause button. It is of course possible to resume a game after a disconnection, but the extra time given to one side or another might be a massive advantage. There is also no way to guarantee that a person that disconnected doesn't consult an engine while they are offline. Saint Louis chose the most standard approach to this problem: you disconnect, you lose.

It wouldn't be unreasonable to think that during a five-day tournament none of the ten participants would disconnect any of their games, but an important disconnection happened already on the first day. In some ways it made the tournament more exciting, and in other ways it felt like a bucket of cold water: how seriously can you take this tournament as a fan? It's hard to get emotionally invested in an event where someone can score a goose egg for such a random reason.

The tournament started hot as Magnus Carlsen defeated his main internet rival:

Hikaru Nakamura
Magnus Carlsen
St. Louis rapid 2020 (1)

position after 23.♕e4

White has sacrificed a pawn to create threats against the enemy king. g4 might be possible, but also sacrifices

Most tournaments that are held online must do a bit of prayer to the internet gods. Those gods had other plans, even from day one

on f7 are on tap. Magnus comes up with a nice resource.

23...♘d5!

23...♕xa2 24.g4 hxg4 25.h5 is for the silicone beasts to hold: 25...♕b2!!, and Black keeps chances of winning, but this is strictly for the TCEC [Top Chess Engine Championship – ed.].

24.♔h1?

One slow move, but that's all it takes. 24.g4 ♕b6+ 25.♔h1 ♕e3 is too late for White: 26.gxh5 ♕xe4 27.♘xe4 gxh5, and in view of the fork on e3, the c4-pawn is still untouchable.

Best was 24.♖xc4! ♘e3 25.♕xe3 ♕xc4 26.♘e4, and the dark-square weaknesses guarantee White at least enough compensation. White can bail out with a perpetual (♘f6xh5) at any point, although he actually can't hope for more.

24...c3 25.♖c2 Panic. The move doesn't do much in terms of the attack, and Black consolidates.

25...♖c8 26.♕f3 ♕a4 27.♖f2 c2 28.♖c1 ♖c3 The rest is easy.

29.♕e2 ♕xb4 30.♔h2 ♖xg3 31.♔xg3 ♕a3+ 32.♔h2 ♕xc1 33.♕c4 ♖c7 34.♕b5 ♕xg5
White resigned.

There was more drama in the second round, when Magnus faced Ian Nepomniachtchi.

Magnus Carlsen
Ian Nepomniachtchi
St. Louis rapid 2020 (2)
English Opening

1.c4 e5 2.g3 ♘c6 3.♗g2 h5!

Why not? Nepo complicates things from the get-go.

4.♘c3

4.♘f3 e4 5.♘g1 is probably very good for White once you start analysing it, but it's hard to come up with this over the board. Or over the lichess interface. Or whatever.

4...h4 5.e3 ♘f6 6.♘ge2 h3 7.♗f3 e4!

It's in the spirit of the position, and in a 25+5 game it doesn't matter what the objective evaluation of this move is. I'm still giving it an exclamation mark.

8.♘xe4 ♘e5 9.♘2c3 ♘xc4

9...♘d3+ 10.♔f1 is just a check.

10.♘xf6+ ♕xf6

11.♘d5

11.0-0 would probably have led to a huge advantage for White. He can just

start pushing his central pawns, gain massive amounts of space, and later exert pressure against the weakened h3-pawn. Black simply can't contest with something like ...c6-d5: his king is still in the middle of the board, after all. I do believe there was something psychological going on throughout the tournament – some players just didn't want to play 'normally'.

11...♕d6 12.d4 c6 13.♘c3 ♕b4?
Black wants to play ...d5, although putting the queen basically anywhere else was more prudent.

14.a3 ♕a5 15.0-0 d5 16.e4 dxe4

17.♗xe4? 17.♖e1 ♗e6 18.♖xe4 0-0-0 19.♕e2! doesn't appear to be as strong from afar, but once you reach this position, it is clear that Black's running out of ways to hold his position together: 19...♗d5 20.♘xd5 cxd5 21.♖f4, and White should win.

17...♗e6

18.d5? Over-optimistic. 18.♕e2 ♗e7 19.♖d1 still looks better for White, with b4 and d5 on the menu.

18...cxd5 19.♗xd5
19.♘xd5 0-0-0 20.b4 ♕b5 21.♘c3 is a computeresque way of getting out of more serious problems.

Online drama. While his game against Ian Nepomniachtchi is still far from decided, Magnus Carlsen begins to realize that he has disconnected.

When the situation turns against you, some decisions sometimes seem more justified than they are. Better was 27...♖xe6! 28.♖ac1 ♖c6 29.♖fe1 ♖xc1 30.♖xc1 ♕e6, and even if Black loses his queenside, as long as his king reaches safety on the kingside, that h3-pawn will provide plenty of counterplay.

28.♗e5 ♗f6 29.♗xf6 0-0 30.♕g4 ♖xf6 31.♕xh3

Black's lost a pawn, but he does have plenty of activity. Behind it, his structure is still bad.

31...♖c2 32.b4 ♕c6 33.♖ad1 ♕b6 34.♔g2 ♖c3 35.♕e4! ♖xa3 36.♖d2 ♖af3 37.♔g2 a6 38.♖c2 ♖f8

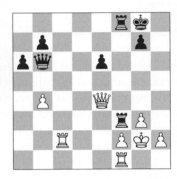

A wild game so far. With both players running out of time, Magnus's position is certainly to be preferred. The pressure on f2 is annoying, but if he can take care of that, his long-term king prospects are a bit better. Right when the commentators were bracing for an interesting finish, Carlsen's screen froze, he lost on time and things were clear: the Internet had claimed another chess game.

Pentala Harikrishna, one of the leaders after Day 1, revealed some of the secrets of online chess: 'I think with online the best preparation is to make sure that your Internet connection is stable and that you don't get disconnected.' This is easier said than done, but the Indian star, who resides in Prague, was actually playing from David Navara's apartment! 'He has better internet'. Hard to argue with that, this day and age.

19...♖d8 20.♕e2 ♖xd5 21.♕xc4
White, for now, keeps Black's king in the centre. Giving up your light-squared bishop in the face of those weaknesses around your king is certainly suspicious, however.

21...♖e5 22.♕d3

22...♕c5?!
22...♕b6! does things very similar to ...♕c5 (threatening ...♕c6, above all), but it also defends the b7-pawn.

23.♕f3!
An important move. White takes control of the h1-a8 diagonal before Black does.

23...♕c8 23...♗e7 24.♗f4 ♖eh5 25.♕xb7 is just very messy.

24.♗f4
Around this moment, Nepo sensed that things had gone wrong, and started shaking his head. His position is still OK, but the initiative has passed to his opponent.

24...♖c5 25.♘e4 ♖c6
25...♕c6 26.♖ac1 (26.♖fc1 miraculously does not fall apart for Black: 26...♗d5) 26...♗d5 27.♖fe1 ♖xc1 28.♖xc1 ♗xe4 29.♕e3 is unclear.

26.♘g5 ♗e7 27.♘xe6

27...fxe6

Wesley on point!

Wesley So is the type of player that is incredibly strong if he gets off to a good start. He is excellent at maintaining a top position in the leader boards, and his style makes it extremely dangerous to take risks against him. Sometimes he fades away from tournaments if he doesn't start strong, but as we can see from the following game, he was on point!

NOTES BY
Wesley So

**Wesley So
Jeffery Xiong**
St. Louis rapid 2020 (1)
Sicilian Defence, Rossolimo Variation

First of all, I would like to extend thanks to Jeanne and Rex Sinquefield for still managing to hold powerful chess events in this Year of the Virus. It gives players hope, something to prepare for in the midst of the craziness! This rapid game was played in the very first round of the St. Louis Rapid and Blitz Tournament.

I have worked a little with Jeffery Xiong in the past, and we were also teammates in the recently concluded Online Olympiad, so I have some experience with him. He is talented and hardworking, and you can see from his results that he slowly improves year after year. Resourcefulness and an ability to spot deep tactics from a mile away are some of his best qualities. I'm sure we'll see more of Jeffery in the future, as he keeps moving up. He is now firmly #5 in the US, so I'm sure many people are excited to have him as a member of the US Olympic team! Hopefully, for that event we will all be sitting across boards. I was pleasantly surprised when they invited Jeffery to be one of the players at this top level tournament (Caruana could not participate because he was playing in the Bundesliga).

1.e4 I like 1.e4, especially online, because it allows me to kind of predict what sort of positions I'm heading into. Also, I'm currently compiling a 1.e4 Lifetime Repertoire for White, and I should be confident enough to play what I recommend against anyone in the world, right?
1...c5 Jeffery played a variety of openings against 1.e4 in this tournament alone. French, Alekhine, Scandinavian, 1...e5 and a variety of Sicilians. Just like Ivanchuk, who plays all sorts of openings. In general, I think he likes testing both himself and his opponent, just investigating different openings. Unlike other top players, his repertoire is not yet fully set.
2.♘f3 Following the usual stuff that White goes for.
2...♘c6 3.♗b5

The Sicilian Rossolimo. It's hard to find anything substantial against the Sveshnikov these days, since the lines are forcing and well-known. With 3.♗b5, on the other hand, White can play more slowly and steer the game more towards strategic and positional play. It's all about the pawn structure and piece play here, compared to the forcing lines of the Sveshnikov.
3...e6
3...g6 is the main line and the most solid, but Jeffery prefers his own ways.
4.0-0 ♘ge7
Here I spent some time thinking, as I've played 5.d4 against him before. Meanwhile, the other two critical options are 5.♖e1 and 5.c3.
5.d4
In the end, I just decided to see what he had in mind against the same line.

5...cxd4 6.♘xd4
We get a Sicilian Open type of position with my bishop on b5 and his knight badly placed on e7.
6...♕b6 7.♘xc6 bxc6
I always thought that 7...dxc6 is the more solid option, at least keeping pawn symmetry and Black going for a quick ...♘g6/...♗e7, followed by castling kingside.

8.♗d3
8.♗e2 is the other option, keeping control of the d4-square. I think that's what I played against him during training. But I wanted to deviate just a little bit and see what he had in the other line. So I withdrew my bishop to the more active square d3.
8...♘g6 9.c4 ♗c5 10.♘c3 ♗d4
With the bishop on e2, this plan would not have been possible.

11.♘e2
I could also start with 11.♖b1 right away, but it does not hurt to repeat moves once.
11...♗c5 12.♖b1
This makes the position of his bishop on c5 uncomfortable, since I am threatening b2-b4.
12...a5 13.♘c3 ♗d4 14.♘a4

Wesley So in his comfortable home office in the company of 'a bossy old cat', 18-year-old Zanzibar.

14...♕c7

If 14...♕a7 White can sacrifice a pawn with 15.c5, breaking the coordination of Black's pieces, and if he takes the pawn, I get a quick ♗e3, followed by f2-f4, with the initiative.

15.c5

This prevents ....c6-c5, and cuts off the supply lines of his bishop in the centre.

15...0-0 16.♖e1

Preparing ♗e3, to get rid of his powerful bishop in the centre. I remember seeing this idea in my preparation and it looks quite natural. Now he has some problems with his bishop.

16...d6

Trying to support his bishop; very logical.

17.♗e3 Less accurate is 17.cxd6 ♕xd6 18.♗e3, because Black has 18...c5, when he will be able to support his centre, and if I take on d4, he will recapture with the pawn: 19.♗xd4 cxd4.

17...dxc5

Slightly more accurate is 17...♗xe3 18.♖xe3 ♖d8. That way my knight is still badly placed on the side-lines.

18.♘xc5 ♖d8 19.♗xd4 ♖xd4

20.♕c2

White can be pleased with the outcome of the opening. The knight on c5 is powerful, and we are ready to challenge for control of the d-file. Black's queenside pawns are isolated, and he does not have enough time to support his rook on d4. His bishop on c8 has no good squares.

20...e5 21.♖bd1 Preparing ♗c4.

21...♘f8 22.♗c4

Now for better or worse, Black should probably try 22...♘e6, just accepting the doubled pawns. In return he is able to support his active rook on d4. But in a rapid game that's a very difficult decision to make.

22...♕e7 23.♖xd4 exd4 24.♘d3

Probably not the most accurate, but I like this natural move. White solidly blockades his pawns, meanwhile preparing to start an attack with f2-f4.

24...♗g4 I was very surprised with

this move. Where is the bishop going? 24...♗e6 would have saved a tempo.

25.f4 Threatening to trap his bishop with f4-f5. Jeffery now has to pull the emergency brake and save his bishop.

25...♗e6 26.f5 ♗xc4 27.♕xc4

27...♕d7 This loses a pawn. Much more tenacious is 27...♕f6!, which we had probably missed or underestimated. My pawns on e4 and f5 are halted temporarily and he creates fast counterplay with ...♖e8. White's going to have to continue accurately to preserve his advantage.

28.♘e5 Seizing the opportunity and exploiting his mistake. That's what fast games are about!

28...♕c7 29.♕xd4

29.♕xc6 is even easier. If the queens are traded, White will get a winning endgame, thanks to Black's inactive knight on f8.

29...♖d8

30.♕c5 30.♕c3 is even stronger, since it avoids ...♘d7. White will possibly grab a second pawn on the queenside.

30...♘d7 I forgot that he now has ...♕b6, check, in reply to 31.♕e7.

31.♘xd7 ♖xd7 32.e5 ♖d5

33.♕e3 ♕e7 Black is still a pawn down, but at least he's managed to trade off his passive knight on f8.

34.h3 With hindsight, the easier option was 34.♕g3, to keep the queens on the board. I don't think Black will be able to survive the coming onslaught with f6 or e6.

34...♕c5 I guess Black has more saving chances in a rook ending, because then he would at least not have to worry about the safety of his king.

35.♔h2 ♕xe3 36.♖xe3 ♔f8

His king is quickly becoming active, so I played:

37.f6!

Which ruins his pawn structure and keeps his king locked out in the back rank for now.

My first intention was 37.♖e2, but I got a bit worried about 37...♔e7 (37...f6 38.exf6 gxf6 39.g4 allows White to keep good winning chances, and after 37...h5 I have 38.♔g3 ♖d4 39.♔f3, activating my king, when 39...h4 is not

---

International Correspondence Chess Federation
Official Website | www.iccf.com

Play with the world's best correspondence chess players on one of the most advanced chess servers in the world.

Register at: **www.iccf-webchess.com**

Join a team of thousands playing great chess at ICCF.

ICCF also offers World Championships, Olympiads, and many other Team and Individual Tournaments where you can participate from any place around the globe.

View live games of the world's best players – also free games downloads.

Contact us at: **www.iccf.com**

possible due to 40.♖e4) 38.♔g3 g6, but I guess I can still make progress after 39.♔f4. All my pawns are solidly protected and my king gets active just in time.

37...gxf6 38.exf6

Now all his pawns are split, and if I could win one of his queenside pawns in return for f6, I would get a winning rook ending.

38...♖d2 39.♖e5

The computer suggests 39.♖b3 as the most forceful option. After 39...♔e8 40.♔g3 I manage to activate my king quickly. After 40...a4 41.♖b4 White will be able to create a passed pawn on the queenside.

39...♖xb2 40.♖xa5 ♔e8

Black is defending very well. Obviously I need to hang on to my a-pawn in order to keep winning chances.

41.♔g3 c5 42.a4 ♔d7

This is a mistake, made with little time on the clock. I think he had barely a minute left at this point. His real target should be my a-pawn, not f6. In that regard, 42...c4 or 42...♖a2 would have been more stubborn.

43.♖xc5 ♔e6 White should be technically winning now, since my

Jeffery Xiong is now firmly number 5 in the US, so I'm sure many people are excited to have him as a member of the US Olympic team!

a-pawn is well supported. For example, 44.a5 ♔xf6 45.♔f3 should be enough. But I was trying to hang on my f6-pawn for now.

44.♖c6+ ♔f5 45.a5 ♖a2 46.a6

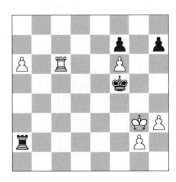

46...♖a4 46...h5 47.♔f3 h4 48.♔e3 would not have changed the outcome of the game, since I will slide my king over to the queenside, and 48...♖xg2 will be met by 49.♖c5+, followed by ♖a5.

47.♔f3 ♖a3+ 48.♔e2 h5 49.♔d2 ♖a2+ 50.♔c3 ♖xg2 51.♖c5+ ♔xf6 52.♖a5

Supporting my passed a-pawn from behind ensures the win.

52...♖g8 53.a7 ♖a8 54.♔c4 h4 55.♔b5 ♔e5 56.♔b6+ ♔f4 57.♔b7 ♖f8 58.a8♕ ♖xa8

59.♔xa8 In fact, this is bad technique, although I had calculated that this was also sufficient for a win.

But in such positions you should always take with the rook – 59.♖xa8. White is effectively saving a tempo, since my king is one step closer to the kingside, and it does not matter where my rook is placed.

59...♔g3

If 59...f5, 60.♔b7 ♔e4 61.♖a4+, followed by ♖xh4, and wins.

60.♖a3+ ♔g2 61.♔b7

My king quickly returns to the kingside – just in time.

61...f5 62.♔c6 f4 63.♔d5 f3 64.♔e4 f2 65.♖f3

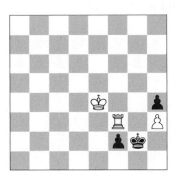

The pawn ending is just winning, and Black has no more tricks left.

65...f1♕ 66.♖xf1 ♔xf1 67.♔f3!
Black resigned.

I usually like to give a little insight into the country, city or venue I am playing in... Well, I can tell you that I have a very comfortable office in my home. This quiet space is dedicated to my work and there are no distractions... except for a bossy old cat which gets offended when the door is closed and howls until I let him in!

■ ■ ■

Another player who, like Harikrishna, was not playing from his home was Levon Aronian. Levon, kind of amazingly, was playing for Baden-Baden during the mornings in Germany, and moonlighted online as a rapid and blitz player. Despite having two jobs at the same time, Levon's results were good and some of his games were wild.

It would be strange to have a tournament nowadays in which Carlsen isn't leading, so he fixed that by scoring 3/3 on Day 2, including the following lovely win against Leinier Dominguez.

NOTES BY
Peter Heine Nielsen

Leinier Dominguez
Magnus Carlsen
St Louis rapid 2020 (5)
Philidor Defence

1.e4 e5 2.♘f3 d6!?

Double homage paid: to the father of understanding the importance of pawn structure in chess, Philidor, but also to Daniil Dubov, who recently revived the opening named after the great Frenchman.
3.d4 exd4 4.♘xd4 ♘f6 5.♘c3 ♗e7 6.♗f4
White obviously has a lot of decent set-ups, but this is the most ambitious one, aiming for opposite castling.
6...0-0 7.♕d2 c6 8.0-0-0 b5 9.f3 b4

10.♘b1?!
The computer gives 10.♘a4 as much better for White. In an interview, Dubov was asked about the fact that the computer said the Philidor was better for White, and he answered along the lines of: 'Yes, I can also read what the computer says.'
10...a5 11.g4 a4 12.h4 c5

Black might not look so well-placed for a pawn-storm, but first of all, there is no alternative to a race to the enemy king, and secondly, Black's pawns are closer to the target, and the b1-knight is out of play.
13.♘f5 ♗xf5 14.gxf5 ♘c6 15.h5 ♘d4 16.♕g2 ♔h8

Maybe the key position in the game. Seeing what happens in the game,

and not to mention AlphaZero, 17.h6!? looks obvious for White now. But Black has the stunning reply 17...g5!!.

ANALYSIS DIAGRAM

Taking the pawn with either the bishop or the queen loses to 18...♖g8. 18.♗e3 is best, but 18...♘d7, followed by 19...♗f6, starts a strong counter-attack on the dark squares, while at the same time completely securing the black king. So the fact that White wins a pawn on d4 is of very little relevance.
17.c3 is the computer move, when after 17...bxc3 18.bxc3 ♕b6 Black gets a strong attack for the sacrificed piece.
17.♗e3 h6!
Game over! Black's king now is completely safe, and will remain so, while Black starts taking swings at the white monarch. If 18.♖g1 then 18...♖g8 simply defends and White has no reasonable way to continue his attack.
18.♗d3 ♘d7 19.♖hg1 ♗f6 20.f4 ♖e8

The computer's evaluation is fascinating: -3! Despite material equality,

Black's attack means he is completely winning.

**21.♗xd4 cxd4 22.♘d2 ♘c5
23.♘c4 b3 24.♔b1 bxc2+
25.♗xc2 ♖b8 26.♗d3**

26...♖b4?

Magnus should have kept it simple, just reinforcing his position with moves like 26...♕c7 and 26...♕e7. Now things suddenly become concrete, and White gets a chance.

**27.a3 ♖b3 28.♗c2 ♖b8 29.e5!
dxe5 30.fxe5 ♖xe5 31.♘xe5
♗xe5**

Black obviously is fine, and has a position that is easier to play and a

With little time on the clock, Magnus had to find a beautiful combination, but the World Champion delivered when needed

Leinier Dominguez fell victim to a beautiful combination.

king that is safer; but Dominguez is very much back in the game.

**32.♗d3 ♗f6 33.♕c2 ♕a5
34.♖g2 ♘xd3 35.♕xd3 ♕d5
36.♖e2 ♔h7 37.♕e4??**

Returning the favour. With little time on the clock, Magnus had to find a beautiful combination, but the World Champion delivered when needed:

37...♖xb2+!! 38.♔xb2 d3+
The bishop's primary task was

perhaps to defend the g7-pawn, but all along it was pointing in the direction of White's king, with its potential now being released.

**39.♔c1 ♕c5+ 40.♔d2 ♕c2+
41.♔e1 ♗h4+!**

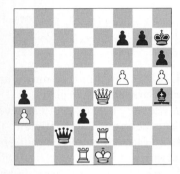

The sting in the tail. If 42.♕xh4, then 42...♕xe2 is mate, and 42.♔f1 ♕xd1+ also wins trivially, so White resigned.

■ ■ ■

The separation between the eventual tournament winners and the rest of the field started on Day 3, the last day of the Rapid. Carlsen showed excellent Nimzo-Indian understanding:

**Alireza Firouzja
Magnus Carlsen**
St. Louis rapid 2020 (7)

position after 12...♗a6

Black has a decent position. He is about to get rid of the bishop pair and is preparing the counter in the centre with ...e5 or ...c5 or both.

13.c4?

Inexperience. Firouzja relies on his bishop pair too much, and holds on to his pawn centre.

13...c5! These kinds of moves are particularly difficult to play.

13...♕xd2+ 14.♗xd2 c5 15.a5 gives White counterplay, sufficient to distract Black from fully engaging on the centre.

14.♘e2 After 14.♕xa5 bxa5, despite the ripped structure on the queenside, the quick development by Black and the pressure on the central files will cause White real headaches: 15.♘e2 ♘c6 16.♗a3 ♘b4!, for example, is quite unpleasant.

14...♘c6 15.♔f2 ♘b4

15 moves in, and White's position is nearly hopeless. He doesn't have a good way to handle the defence of the c4-pawn.

16.♗b2 cxd4 17.♘xd4

17.exd4 ♖ac8 18.♖hc1 ♘fd5! is just one example of how bad White's position is: 19.♔g1 ♘xd3 20.♕xd3 ♕b4, winning.

17...♖ad8! 18.♗c3 ♘xd3+ 19.♕xd3 ♕c5 Black has the material and the compensation, and the rest was a breeze for Carlsen.

20.♕c2 ♗xc4 21.♖hd1 ♘d5 22.♗d2 e5 23.♘f5 ♘f4 24.♔g3 ♘d3 25.♕c3 ♗e6 26.♕xc5 ♘xc5 White resigned.

A cat named Zanzibar

Meanwhile, Wesley So was busy climbing the standings. As said, Wesley traditionally has a timid approach to tournaments, but given just a bit of rope he is very capable of playing flawless chess. He finished the rapid portion with two wins on different sides of the ♖e1 variation of the Berlin Defence! This will probably be the first and last time you ever read such a sentence. Wesley was playing from his home in Minnetonka, Minnesota, where he lives with his family. The member of his family that was a literal show stopper, however, was beautiful Zanzibar. At 18 years of age, Zanzibar is just a gorgeous cat and deserved all of the camera time he got and more. I don't remember the last time a cat jumped into the lap of a participant of the Grand Chess Tour during a game, but this is 2020.

The Blitz

With the first blitz day under way, it was clear that the two leaders had very different approaches. After losing his first game against Jeffery Xiong, Wesley So was able to bounce back in the third against Ian Nepomniachtchi. Then, deciding that he had taken enough risks for the moment, Wesley played super-solid chess to finish the day with six consecutive draws.

Magnus Carlsen meanwhile seemed to have a dramatic game every single round. His ambition for finding complications seems to know no limits, but it landed him in hot water quite often. This type of rollercoaster chess makes it awesome to follow these events. You could argue that Magnus was lucky more than once, but you could also argue that the World Champion makes his own luck. Just take a look at this incredible escape against Alireza Firouzja.

Alireza Firouzja
Magnus Carlsen
St. Louis blitz 2020 (7.1)

position after 37.♘g4

We're in the middle of a wild game. Black's rooks look threatening, but a closer inspection reveals that they're pretty uncoordinated, since the knight on g4 is taking care of business. Meanwhile, the c7-pawn is really hanging.

37...♗d6 38.♗g3

38.♕c4!, and sacrificing on c7 quickly finishes the game, as f6 and b6 will be impossible to defend.

38...♖3h7 39.♕b2 ♕e7 40.♖1c4?

40...♗h5 40...♗e8 captured an important rook. **41.♕c3** The Alekhine Gun was unnecessary, but it's certainly aesthetic.

41...♗xg4 42.♖xc7! ♗h3+ 43.♔f2 ♗xc7 44.♖xc7 ♔h6 45.♖xe7 ♖xe7 46.d6 ♖d7 47.♗xe5! fxe5 48.♕xe5

You could argue that Magnus was lucky more than once, you could also argue that the World Champion makes his own luck

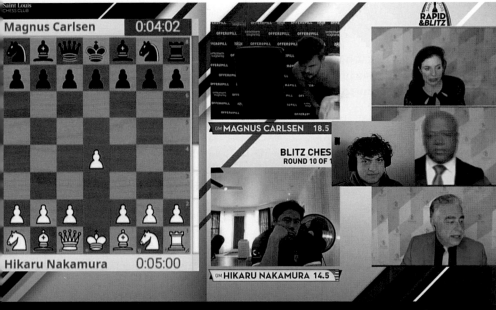

A pretty awkward moment. Hikaru Nakamura tries to keep a straight face as Magnus Carlsen, not yet dressed, is clearly unaware that the game has already started.

Excellent show so far by Alireza. This powerful sacrifice gives him a bunch of passed pawns, and coupled with the weakness of the black king on h6, this is really game over. But Carlsen has that World Champion magic that makes him very slippery.

48...♔h7 49.♕f6?! 49.♕e6! ♖g7 50.♔g3 ♗f1 51.f6 is much cleaner.
49...♖g8 50.e5 ♖gg7! 51.♔g3 ♖df7!

Out of nowhere, Black has organized counterplay against the f5-pawn just on time. Alireza panics, but in a blitz game with the seconds ticking down, it is difficult to find the winning continuation.

52.♕d8? 52.♕xf7!, and the pawns finish the game: 52...♖xf7 53.♔xh3 ♖xf5 54.d7 ♖f8 (or 54...♖xf3+ 55.♔g4 ♖d3 56.e6, and wins) 55.e6, and wins.

52...♗xf5 53.♕e8
Panic. White is threatening e6, but this is easily repelled.

53...♗d7 54.♕a8 ♖g6 55.♕b7 ♖e6

White's pawns are blocked and the huge material advantage begins to manifest itself. Carlsen does not give him another opportunity.

56.♕e4+ ♔g7 57.♕e3 ♖f5

58.♕xb6 ♖exe5 59.♕a7 ♖f7 60.♕d4 ♔f6 61.b4 axb4 62.♕xb4 ♔g6 63.a5 ♖e3 64.a6 ♖exf3+ 65.♔g2 ♖f2+ 66.♔g1 ♖f1+ 67.♔g2 ♗c6+ 68.♔g3 ♖7f3+ 69.♔h2 ♖3f2+ 70.♔g3 ♖g2+ And mate. White resigned.

The day didn't always go his way, and with losses to Nepomniachtchi and Harikrishna, Carlsen only scored enough to take the lead over So by half a point.

Keep your shirt on
The final day started with one of the clowniest things I've seen in chess. Magnus arrived late for his first game against Nakamura, and although on the broadcast his clock started to tick down, his clock was not actually ticking. Magnus peaked from the side, shirtless, akin to a football fan that just got out of the shower checking to see if the kick off had already occurred. Noticing that it had, he probably realized he didn't have time to grab a beer and a snack so he quickly threw on a shirt, made a move and disappeared off camera to readjust.

In my opinion, if Nakamura complained that Carlsen went off camera during the game it would have been hard to argue against an immediate forfeit. For the competition's sake I'm glad that instead Nakamura just crushed him on the chessboard.

Hikaru Nakamura
Magnus Carlsen
St Louis blitz 2020 (10.2)
Sicilian Defence, Kan Variation

1.e4
Due to the way lichess clocks work, time does not actually start ticking until both players make a move. Chris Callahan has informed us that the option to start the clocks at a specified time has now been implemented on lichess to avoid these kinds of situation, and to make tournaments run more smoothly.

1...c5 2.♘f3 e6 At this point, Carlsen was down only one minute on the clock; truly a small penalty. **3.d4 cxd4 4.♘xd4 a6 5.♗d3 ♗c5 6.♘b3 ♗a7 7.♕e2 ♘c6 8.♗e3 d6 9.0-0 ♘f6 10.♘c3 0-0 11.♖ad1 b5 12.f4?**

12...e5

12...♗xe3+ 13.♕xe3 ♘g4 14.♕h3 ♕b6+ 15.♔h1 ♘e3 is not the kind of sequence these players tend to miss, but clearly both were a bit rattled. **13.♗xa7 ♖xa7 14.f5 ♖d7 15.♘d5 ♗b7 16.c4 bxc4 17.♗xc4**

17...♘e7?
Kind of an insane move.

18.♘xf6+ gxf6 19.♔h1 ♔h8 20.♖d3 It's not a big surprise that Black is close to getting mated here.

20...♗xe4?? 20...♖c7 21.♖h3 ♖g8! is still a fight. **21.♕xe4 d5 22.♕h4** The bishop is taboo due to ♖h3, but also because of ♕xf6+. It's even hard to say what Carlsen had missed. **22...♘g8 23.♖g3** Black resigned.

After the tournament Carlsen mentioned he had had too little time before the round. It makes you wonder how seriously some of these players are taking this event. Why are there so many other things going on during a tournament day?

For Carlsen of course there is no easier way to enter beast mode than to lose a game. It's like an instant light switch flip, and he had a strong showing after that. His game against Wesley So was, of course, crucial and he managed to win that one.

Further wins against Harikrishna and Xiong would normally have been enough to seal the deal, but not this time. Inspiration truly comes

from the most random places sometimes, and for Wesley So it came after Ian Nepomniachtchi suspiciously declined a draw:

Wesley So
Ian Nepomniachtchi
St. Louis blitz 2020 (4.1)
Grünfeld Indian Defence, Exchange Variation

1.d4 ♘f6 2.c4 g6 3.♘c3 d5 4.cxd5 ♘xd5 5.e4 ♘xc3 6.bxc3 ♗g7 7.♘f3 c5 8.♖b1 0-0 9.♗e2 ♗g4 10.♖xb7 ♗xf3? A mistake; or at least that is what it looks like to me. 10...♘c6 is some kind of mess. **11.♗xf3 cxd4** Nepo is happily repeating the 14-move draw that these two players had in the 2019 Tata Steel Blitz. It also looks as if neither of their seconds has noticed that White does not have to recapture on d4.

12.cxd4? 12.e5! d3 (12...dxc3 13.♕xd8 ♖xd8 14.♗b3 ♗a6 15.♗xa8 ♖xa8 16.♖xc3 ♗xe5 is not tenable) 13.♖b1 is +3, according to my engine. Maybe Nepo found a way to get great compensation from here, but I'm more inclined to believe my processor. **12...♗xd4 13.0-0 ♘c6 14.♕a4**

This is where the previous game

St. Louis 2020 Rapid & Blitz								
				elo rapid	elo blitz	rapid	blitz1	blitz2	total
1	Magnus Carlsen	IGM	USA	2881	2886	12	6½	5½	24
	Wesley So	IGM	USA	2741	2816	13	5	6	24
3	Hikaru Nakamura	IGM	USA	2829	2900	9	5½	6½	21
4	Alexander Grischuk	IGM	RUS	2784	2765	10	4½	4	18½
	Levon Aronian	IGM	ARM	2778	2739	9	3½	6	18½
6	Ian Nepomniachtchi	IGM	RUS	2778	2785	10	5	3	18
7	Jeffery Xiong	IGM	USA	2730	2724	7	4½	4	15½
	Pentala Harikrishna	IGM	IND	2705	2614	9	3½	3	15½
9	Leinier Dominguez	IGM	USA	2786	2654	6	3½	3	12½
	Alireza Firouzja	IGM	FRA	2703	2770	5	3½	4	12½
9 rounds of rapid + 18 rounds of blitz - double points for rapid									

finished with a handshake. White is slightly better on account of his bishop pair, and this kind of risk-free positions are Wesley So's dream scenario.

14...♖c8 15.♗a3 ♗b6?

Immediately going wrong. 15...♗f6 16.♖d1 ♕a5 is not great, but at least after 17.♕xa5 ♘xa5 18.♖xa7 ♘c6 19.♖a6 it seems White still has technical problems ahead of him to convert.

16.♖d1 ♕e8

17.♗e2! Such a lovely retreat! Once the bishop gets to b5, there will be no good way to break the pin on the diagonal. Nepo jettisons his queen before succumbing to the pressure.

17...♘a5 18.♗b5 ♘xb7 19.♗xe8 ♖fxe8

The game is far from clearly winning, but Wesley continued to exert pressure until Nepo collapsed, in an excellent display of technique despite the blitz time-control.

20.g3 ♘c5 21.♗xc5 ♗xc5 22.♔g2 ♖ed8 23.♖xd8+ ♖xd8 24.♕c2 ♗b6 25.a4 e5 26.h4 h5 27.f3 ♗e3 28.♕c3 ♗d4 29.♕c7 ♖e8 30.a5 ♖e6 31.f4 ♔g7 32.♔f3

Nakamura's increased online presence brings him the big bucks; throwing in a game for the memes and the laughs is probably suited for his Twitch audience

♖f6 33.♕d7 ♗c3 34.♕xa7 exf4 35.gxf4 ♗e5 36.♕e3

36...♗c7 37.♕c3 ♗b8 38.a6 ♗a7 39.f5 gxf5 40.exf5 ♗b8 41.♔e4 ♗a7 42.♕b2 ♗b6 43.♕c3 ♗f2 44.♔f4

Black resigned.

The Bongcloud

Trailing by one point with two rounds to go, Wesley more or less forced himself to try to win the last two. Nakamura was trailing him by a full two points. After Wesley beat Aronian in the penultimate round, third place was guaranteed for Nakamura with a chance still for first place for Carlsen or So.

In the last round, Nakamura used the Bongcloud against Xiong. For those that are blissfully unaware of what that is in chess terms, it is the meme that 1.e4 e5 (or any) 2.♔e2 is extremely strong. There is a minor (but wrong) argument that 1.f3 e5 (or any) 2.♔f2 is the real Bongcloud. Nadal was recently asked in a press conference about his opponent serving underhand against him. I thought

Nadal's answer was rather eloquent, stating that it was part of the game and only the player that did it would know if it was done for the correct reason: are you using every rule available to you to confuse the opponent or are you intentionally being disrespectful just for the sake of it?

In this case only Nakamura knows what was going on through his mind, but truthfully the game did not matter for him at all since the event wasn't even rated. Xiong eventually lost. Nakamura's increased online presence brings him the big bucks; throwing in a game for the memes and the laughs is probably suited for his Twitch audience. The faster we get to over the board chess, the happier I will be.

Simply outstanding

Back to the winners. A final trick against Harikrishna in the last round allowed Wesley So to catch Magnus Carlsen who drew his final game. In previous editions of the Saint Louis Rapid and Blitz, a tiebreak would quickly follow to determine the champion of the event. This tournament did not have tiebreaks at the end. There was no particular reason for that this year. As an organizer I know that lichess does not handle Armageddons, and there might have been a possibility to avoid headaches by not including a playoff. This angered some fans, but for a tournament that had 27 rounds of chess if there is no clear winner I am fine with splitting the top prize. It's an internet tournament, after all.

The performance of both players was simply outstanding, and despite their completely different angles used to approach the tournament, they were very successful at it. Magnus, as always, reminded the audience that had he not disconnected against Nepo in Round 2 he would have won the tournament, but he also took time to praise So's excellent play. Magnus can take the moral victory, Wesley will always be just fine sharing first. ∎

MAXIMize
your Tactics
with Maxim Notkin

Find the best move in the positions below

Solutions on page 89

1. White to move

2. White to move

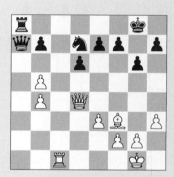

3. White to move

4. Black to move

5. White to move

6. White to move

7. White to move

8. White to move

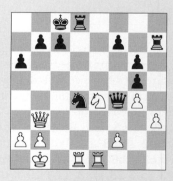

9. White to move

GIBRALTAR

The Women's FIDE Grand Prix
is coming to Gibraltar!

GRAND PRIX

GIBRALTAR, JANUARY 17 — 29, 2021

Hosted At The Caleta Hotel

HM Government of Gibraltar

 **TOTAL**

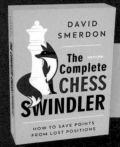

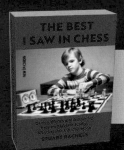

Thomas Willemze

Club players, test your decision-making skills!

What would you play?

How to decide on complex pawn moves

One of the first 'chess rules' I learned was to answer an attack on the flank with a counter-strike in the centre – an indispensable rule for any ambitious chess player, but unfortunately not a guarantee of success. This kind of rule of thumb is important to point you in the right direction, but only practice will help you find the correct pawn moves at the right time in your own games.

To illustrate the importance of such *complex pawn move decisions*, I will discuss the game between Jan Budzinski (1902) and Michal Chmielecki (1761), in which White was aiming for a kingside attack right from the start and Black had to find the correct pawn moves in response.

The exercises

I selected the four most important decisions for Black and present them to you as exercises. They can be quite challenging, which is why I advise you to take your time and only write

Only write down your answer if you would be willing to play the move in an actual game

down your answer if you would be willing to play the move in an actual game.

Exercise 1

position after 10.♘e2

White has put his mind on the f4-f5 push. **What would you play?** Block the f-pawn with **10...f7-f5**, react in the centre with **10...d7-d5**, or ignore the threat with **10...b7-b6**?

Exercise 2

position after 14.♗d3

The f4-f5 push is still in the air. It is again your turn. Would you block the f-pawn with **14...f7-f5**, close the centre with **14...e6-e5**, or ignore the threat with **14...♗b7** ?

Exercise 3

position after 16.g4

The white pawn has made it to f5, and Black must anticipate the threatened attack on his king. **What would you play?** Block the pawn with **16...f6**, or release the tension with **16...gxf5** ?

Exercise 4

position after 17.♘g3

What would you play? Close the door with **17...g5**, or maintain the tension with **17...♗b7** ?

I hope you enjoyed these complex pawn move decisions. You can find the full analysis of this game and advice on making the correct pawn moves below.

Jan Budzinski (1902)
Michal Chmielecki (1761)
Sekocin Stary, Polish U14
Championship 2010
Sicilian Defence, Grand Prix Attack

1.e4 c5 2.♘c3 ♘c6 3.f4 g6 4.♘f3 ♗g7 5.♗c4 e6 6.d3 ♘ge7 7.0-0 0-0 8.♕e1 This is a very typical move in this set-up. The queen is on its way to h4 to launch an attack. **8...♘d4 9.♘xd4 cxd4 10.♘e2**

White started the game ambitiously and has clearly pinned his hopes on f4-f5 to increase the scope of his pieces. Even though Black knows what is coming, he is still facing a difficult choice. You might have experienced this when solving **Exercise 1**. The correct move was:

10...d5!

Black follows one of the oldest rules in chess and answers an attack on the flank with a firm response in the centre. There was no time to wait any longer, since the patient 10...b6 allows 11.f5!, giving White the kind of game he was gunning for.

ANALYSIS DIAGRAM

11...exf5 12.♗g5!. This important move prevents 12...d5 and leads to a

very powerful attack. Note that White will regain the f-pawn soon, since 12...fxe4 loses a piece after 13.♕h4!.

The alternative 10...f5 was also playable, since Black can meet 11.e5 ♘c6 12.♕f2 with 12...d6!.

ANALYSIS DIAGRAM

This pawn break is crucial for Black, as it reactivates the dark-squared bishop and puts enough pressure on the centre to keep the game on an even keel.

11.♗b3! White correctly maintains the tension in the centre. 11.exd5 ♘xd5 would ruin his f4-f5 ambitions and give Black an easy game.

11...dxe4 12.dxe4 b6

13.♗c4!

It was important for Black to recognize the danger of his passive strategy and look for opportunities to generate counterplay at any cost

With his last move White aims to go to d3 with the bishop. From there, it can simultaneously support the e4-pawn and block the black d-pawn.

13...♕c7

13...♗b7 would have been more flexible, since Black will have to make this move sooner or later anyway, while the queen might turn out to be just as strong on its initial square.

14.♗d3

Black has played well so far, but has to be careful now. He should develop his pieces as quickly as possible and, above all, keep the centre fluid. The correct solution to **Exercise 2** was, therefore, 14...♗b7! 15.♕h4 ♖ac8.

ANALYSIS DIAGRAM

This set-up allows Black to counter White's kingside play with a timely reaction in the centre, for instance: 16.f5 exf5 17.exf5 ♕c6!.

ANALYSIS DIAGRAM

The second option, 14...f5, was inferior. It puts paid to White's attack, but shows a serious drawback after 15.e5.

ANALYSIS DIAGRAM

The dark-squared bishop is completely out of play, and unlike in the variation after 10... f5, Black no longer has the liberating ...d7-d6 break.

The third option was played in the game:

14...e5

After this move, Black no longer has the option of opening the centre, which means that his opponent can focus exclusively on his kingside attack.

15.f5 ♕c6 16.g4

This ambitious pawn move fortifies the f5-pawn but considerably weakens the white king, giving Black an unexpected opportunity to develop serious counterplay. White had safer and stronger options available in 16.♘g3 and 16.♕h4.

ANALYSIS DIAGRAM

16...f6

Black's attempt to close the kingside is a very natural reaction to the coming attack, but it makes for a very passive position. The solution to **Exercise 3** was to punish White for his provocative pawn move with 16...gxf5! 17.gxf5 ♘xf5! 18.exf5 ♗b7! 19.♕g3 ♔h8.

ANALYSIS DIAGRAM

This looks very dangerous for White, for instance after 20.f6 ♖g8! 21.♕h3 e4!. This is a very complex line rarely to be found in a practical game. It was important for Black to recognize the danger of his passive strategy and

look for opportunities to generate counterplay at any cost.

17.♘g3

17...g5

Black's position was already quite difficult to play, but in **Exercise 4** it was essential to preserve the last bit of flexibility and maintain the tension with 17...♗b7.

ANALYSIS DIAGRAM

White is still clearly better here, but at least he has to reckon with plans like ...♔h8 and ...♖g8 and ...gxf5.

With his last two moves, Black has completely fixed the pawn structure on the kingside and deprived himself of any kind of counterplay. Without tension between pawns to worry about, White can put all his energy in finding the right moment for opening the h-file for his major pieces and develop the irresistible attack he had been aiming for.

18. ♗d2

White can relax now, and slowly starts building up his attack. Note that the immediate 18.h4 was also possible, since 18...gxh4 19.♘h5 ♖f7 20.♕xh4 is very unpleasant for Black. His most stubborn defence would be 18...h6, which would probably transpose to the game.

18...♗d7 19. ♕e2 b5

20. ♔f2!

The king no longer has to worry about his safety in view of the fixed pawns and clears the rook's path to h1.

20...h6 21. ♖h1 ♔f7 22.h4 ♖h8

23. ♖h3!

White has the perfect pawn structure for a fight for the open file. 23...gxh4 24.♖xh4 is never really an option, which means he can patiently optimize his major pieces before opening up the h-file.

23...♖ab8 24. ♖ah1

Make sure you always keep the option open of developing counterplay when needed to prevent your opponent from having a free ride in his kingside attack

The pressure along the h-file is already starting to feel very uncomfortable for Black. He has to reckon with hxg5 on every single move, but is unable to enforce anything.

24...a6 25. ♔f1 ♕a8 26. ♘h5 ♖bf8 27. ♕h2 ♖fg8

White is ready and decides to act on his h-file.

28. ♘xg7 ♔xg7 29.hxg5! hxg5 30. ♖h7+

The rook reaches the seventh rank to great effect. The game finishes immediately.

30...♖xh7 31. ♕xh7+ ♔f8 32. ♗b4!

Well played. The black king is now under attack from two different directions.

32...♕e8 33. ♖h6 ♕f7 34. ♕xf7+ ♔xf7 35. ♖h7+ ♖g7 36. ♖xg7+

Black will lose his knight on the next move, and so he resigned.

This game has taught us to keep our pawns as flexible as possible and make sure we have pawn breaks available to alter the structure when required. Make sure you always keep the option open of developing counterplay when needed to prevent your opponent from having a free ride in his kingside attack. ∎

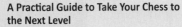

My 100 Best Games
Jan Timman

Covers a career of more than 50 years and includes wins against Karpov, Kasparov, Kortchnoi, Smyslov, Tal, Bronstein, Larsen, Topalov, Spassky and many others.

"This is magnificent. The book is dotted with fascinating anecdotes. Timman plays in a swashbuckling style, but always underpinned with a great strategic and positional sense."
GM Daniel King, Power Play Chess

A Practical Guide to Take Your Chess to the Next Level
Alex Dunne

Defeating 2000+ players will start feeling normal after working with this extended & improved edition of the 1985 bestselling classic. Based on real amateur games, Alex Dunne takes you by the hand and offers lots of practical, straightforward and effective advice. Slowly but surely, you will improve in all aspects of the game. Surprise yourself and reach higher!

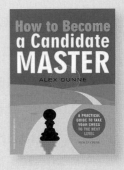

The Tactics Workbook that Also Explains All the Key Concepts
Frank Erwich

"One of the better exercise books to come out in recent years." – *IM John Donaldson*

"An extremely useful training manual. Many club players will benefit." – *IM Herman Grooten, Schaaksite*

"I was very impressed by the range of positions that Erwich selected." – *GM Matthew Sadler*

Ambitious Ideas and Powerful Weapons
Viktor Moskalenko

"Crammed full of opening ideas which will suit players of all strengths. His mix of wit, weapons and wisdom strikes me as the ideal source for anyone seeking inspiration."
GM Glenn Flear

"A host of interesting new and dangerous ideas."
John Upham, British Chess News

A Practical Guide to a Vital Skill in Chess
Merijn van Delft

"Excellent examples. Will have a major impact on your positional progress."
IM Gary Lane, Chess Moves Magazine

"A grandmaster-level skill explained in a comprehensible and readable fashion."
GM Matthew Sadler

"Masterfully discusses a vital topic, to bring your chess to the next level." – *GM Karsten Müller*

Odessky's Sparkling Lines and Deadly Traps
Ilya Odessky

Russian IM Ilya Odessky, the world's leading expert on the 1.b3 and 1...b6 opening systems, presents his findings and achievements of recent years. His baffling traps will help you crush your opponents in the opening, with both White and Black. A highly unusual opening book full of ultra-romantic chess.

"Amazing analysis and great stories. A thoroughly entertaining book." *IM John Donaldson*

Vital Lessons for Every Chess Player
Jesus de la Villa

"If you've never read an endgame book before, this is the one you should start with."
GM Matthew Sadler, former British Champion

"If you really have no patience for endgames, at least read *100 Endgames You Must Know*."
Gary Walters Chess

Improve Your Ability to Spot Typical Mates
Vladimir Barsky

More often than you would expect, positions that look innocent at first sight, turn out to contain a mating pattern.

"An introduction explaining the pattern, some practical examples and then lots of exercises. An instructive book." – *IM Hans Bohm, De Telegraaf*

"A really important book, set out very clearly, extremely well organized." – *GM Daniel King*

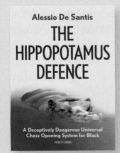

A Deceptively Dangerous Universal Chess Opening System for Black
Alessio De Santis

"Little short of a revelation. De Santis really has come at his subject from all conceivable angles to leave no stone unturned. Did you know that the hippopotamus is the most dangerous of all large animals? In chess opening terms, I would argue that it's also the case." – *GM Glenn Flear*

"Presents a very good view on the many ideas that the Hippopotamus offers." – *IM Dirk Schuh*

Chess Champion of the British Empire
Daniel King

"King has done a simply wonderful job of reanimating the life, times and games of the mysterious Sultan Khan."
Sean Marsh, CHESS Magazine

"A magnificent book. A remarkable chess career captured in the style of a gripping novel."
IM Gary Lane, Chess Moves Magazine

"King offers a lot more than just the games."
Richard James, British Chess News

Half of the 16 teams in the first league gathered in Karlsruhe for the Bundesliga championship tournament. The desire to play 'real chess' again was palpable, and dozens of foreign top players eagerly travelled to Germany. One of them, our reporter **LOEK VAN WELY**, is a Senator these days, but that doesn't mean that the Dutchman can resist the call of the chess pieces.

Baden-Baden continue where they left of

Bundesliga back at the board

At last! The wait had been a long one, but finally, after six months, I would be able to sit at the board again. For half a year I didn't travel abroad, for playing chess or otherwise. I do not want to sound like a whiner, because I know my situation is very different, but I still wondered what it had been like back in the day in the Soviet Union if you were banned from travelling abroad. I recalled a story by Mikhail Gurevich, who was in this unfortunate situation (for different reasons, of course) and so desperate that he jumped at an invitation to play in Mongolia. Don't get me wrong,

Mongolia is high on my bucket list, but I suspect that Misha was hoping to travel to the West instead at the time.

To make the wait even worse, my last official game had been a pretty traumatic experience. In the German Cup, my team of Solingen needed a draw to get into the next round and my team's fate was in my hands. But (of course) I got greedy. Not that I hadn't been warned. On an earlier occasion, my team mate Jan Smeets had been in a similar situation. He also screwed up big time, and ever since I had been teasing him...

Anyway, we were happy to be travelling again. A road trip with the boys, my fellow-countrymen Jorden

van Foreest, Erwin l'Ami and Jan Smeets, was like a trip to heaven. Yes, that bad! As it was, my trip started from The Hague, the Dutch government seat, where I had been attending 'Prinsjesdag'. On the third Tuesday of September, the government reveals their plans for the coming year. In case you have been living under a stone, I got elected to the Dutch Senate or First Chamber in March 2019 (as a member of the political party 'Forum Voor Democratie' – Forum for Democracy – led by Thierry Baudet, who happens to be the great grandson of the brilliant mathematician Henry Baudet, a close friend of Emanuel Lasker's – ed.). Since that time you

In the vast conference centre in Karlsruhe all players of the 8 teams could keep a safe distance as they competed for the Bundesliga trophy.

the shortened Bundesliga would be played on seven consecutive days, was how we had digested six months of forced inactivity. Smeets (who works as a trader) and I agreed that we should have quite an advantage, since being inactive had not changed our status: zombies remain zombies ☺. However, our rivals might have become zombies, too. And isn't that my favourite game: the lame vs. the blind?

It was nice the Germans had managed to pull this event off and organized it so well, taking all the precautions required and creating more than enough space for everyone to play their games safely. Sadly, in the Netherlands, organizing the Dutch Championship for a total of 16 players – eight men and eight women – proved too difficult a task for the Dutch chess federation. In Karlsruhe, in the same congress centre that was used for the Grenke Open, we were playing with a plexiglass screen in the middle of the board, as they did in Biel. So no spitting in your opponent's face this time (although with a curve you could still manage, but less easily), nor launching direct punches. There was a hole at the bottom of the glass in case you had some business on the other side of the board. In Round 6, I had a long queen ending (120 moves), and since I was manoeuvring a lot on the far side of the board, that became pretty annoying. Also, when

have to call me grandmaster Senator Van Wely ☺. Yes, sometimes life takes unexpected turns, and I decided to jump on the bandwagon!

Needless to say, I didn't deserve it, but was it really luck? Anyway, sometimes everything comes together, and the department that I am responsible for is Justice & Security, both very important with regard to Covid-19 legislation. I can tell you that playing chess is easier than politics, you only need to trick *one* opponent! And the best move is the best move, period!

But I must say that after playing chess very intensively for 30 years or so, it's also nice to be doing something else. And in a few years from

now, I might be back! (I haven't really left, but that's how it feels sometimes), so please don't celebrate too early, especially you guys, Jorden van Foreest and Benjamin Bok!

Zombies?

The main question as we arrived in Karlsruhe, where all seven rounds of

Playing chess is easier than politics, you only need to trick *one* opponent!

Loek van Wely in The Hague on 'Prinsjesdag'. In the evening the Grandmaster Senator travelled to Germany to join his team of Solingen.

staring at the 7th and 8th ranks, I was bothered by reflections, but generally speaking the playing conditions were very good.

Two-horse race

As for the championship, it was clear it was going to be a two-horse race with two outspoken favourites: Baden-Baden (with Fabiano Caruana, Maxime Vachier-Lagrave, Levon Aronian, Mickey Adams, Radek Wojtaszek and Richard Rapport) and Viernheim (with Shakhriyar Mamedyarov, Yuriy Kryvoruchko, Anton Korobov, Bassem Amin, David Anton and Vladimir Malakhov). While the rest was just happy to play (speaking for myself!).

In the first round, I couldn't believe my luck when I was going to play my favourite opponent (I have quite a few, but he is top of my list) Romain Edouard (Hamburger SK). I don't know if there is any correlation between him seeing the pairings and suddenly having severe back pains, but the poor guy ended up in

hospital. As a true predator I wanted to visit him there, if only to taunt him a bit, but unfortunately I wasn't allowed to. Anyway Eduardo, I wish you a speedy recovery, but you do owe me those five rating points!

In the second round, Richard Rapport (Baden-Baden) stole the show with his game against Noel Studer (Bayern München).

NOTES BY
Loek van Wely

Noel Studer
Richard Rapport
Bundesliga 2020 (2)
Slav Defence, Stonewall Variation

Welcome to planet Rapport! In my analysis I will try to explain what's happening in this game in three ways: How Mortals like Studer and me think, how the Engine evaluates things and what Richie could possibly have had on his mind ☺.

1.d4 d5 2.c4 e6 3.♘f3 c6 4.♘bd2 f5
Richie: Let's create some imbalance!
5.g3 ♘d7 6.♗g2 ♘h6

Mortal: This looks strange, but the knight is actually pretty good on f7.
7.♕c2 Mortal: Let me postpone castling because you never know with this crazy guy Richie.
7...♘f7 8.b3 g5

Mortal: You see, I was right. There he goes!
9.e3 ♗d6 10.♗b2 a5 11.h4 g4 12.♘g1 0-0 13.♘e2 ♘f6 14.♘f4 ♕e7 15.0-0

Mortal: I think I am safe now. My knight on f4 blocks everything and my pawn structure looks solid. I think I can castle now.

Engine says: if not 15...b5, White will have a large advantage.

15...♘h8 Richie: OK, my plan might be primitive, but is hard to prevent: I am going to sac on f4!

16.c5? Mortal: This move I don't like, but I especially dislike White's next, because it simply ignores (or at least underestimates) Black's plan.

The engine says: 16.a4, followed by either ♕c1/♗a3 or ♘b1/♗a3, would have slowed Black down significantly, especially if White gets to play ♘b1-c3-e2.

16...♗c7 17.a3

Mortal: After this move the situation is out of control and Richie is in his element.

17...♘g6 18.b4 ♘xf4 19.exf4 ♘h5 Mortal: Wait a second, maybe I should pay a bit of attention to my kingside. Positionally, I may be winning, but this is a bit scary.

20.♖fe1 ♘xf4 21.gxf4 ♗xf4

The Engine: 21...♕xh4, with already a large advantage for Black!

22.♘c4!

Mortal: Let's create some counter-play! Engine: I agree!

22...♕xh4 Richie: Let me ignore him!

Richie: OK, my plan might be primitive, but is hard to prevent: I am going to sac on f4!

The engine gives the following as a possible line: 22...dxc4 23.d5 cxd5 24.♗xd5 ♕xh4 25.♖xe6 ♕h2+ 26.♔f1 ♕h3+ 27.♔e1 ♗xe6 28.♗xe6+ ♖f7 29.♗xf7+ ♔f8 30.♕xf5 ♕h1+ 31.♔e2 ♕f3+, and it's a draw.

23.♘b6

Mortal: I am attacking his rook now,

Richard Rapport would have won the Brilliancy Prize if there had been one.

MICHAEL ZAHN

and soon my rook will enter via e6. What could possibly go wrong?

23...e5

Richie: I am going to push my pawns and bring in my bishop from c8. Were you really thinking I was going to move that rook???

24.♘xd5?!

Mortal: I cannot blame Mr. Studer for panicking here.

However, the Engine says: 24.dxe5 ♗h2+ 25.♔f1 f4 26.f3 ♗f5 27.♕c3 axb4 28.axb4 ♖xa1 29.♖xa1 ♗e6 30.♘d7 gxf3 31.♗xf3 ♗g3 32.♖e2 ♗h3+ 33.♔g1 ♕g5 34.♘h1 ♕g6 35.♗b2 ♕b1+ 36.♗c1 ♗xd7 37.e6 ♗e8 38.e7 ♖f7 39.♗h5, and it's equal. Just for your information.

24...cxd5 25.♖xe5

25...♗h2+

Richie thinks White's king is worse on f1 in view of the possible ...f4-f3 push. The Engine says 25...♔g7 or 25...♗d7!.

26.♔f1 ♗xe5 27.♗xd5+ ♔g7 28.dxe5 axb4

Mortal: It looks as if White's initiative is more of an illusion, and in fact he is down material now, with a vulnerable king.

29.♔e2

29...♖xa3?? 29...bxa3 or 29...♖d8, harassing White's bishop, would have done the job, the engine says.

30.♗xa3??
Mortal: My only chance depends on my dark-squared bishop, and I shouldn't exchange it for that miserable rook. Out of principle this moves deserves a double question mark!

Mortal: 30.e6+ ♖c3 (30...♔g6 31.♗xa3 bxa3 32.♖xa3 is equal, the engine says) 31.♗xc3+ bxc3 32.♕xc3+ ♕f6 33.♕xf6+ ♔xf6 looks dead for White. But the tablebase says: 34.♖a8 ♖e8 35.♔f1 ♔e7 36.♗xb7 ♗xe6 37.♖xe8+ ♔xe8 38.f3 h5 39.fxg4 fxg4 40.♔f2 h4 41.♔e3 and draw!

30...bxa3 31.♕c3 f4 32.♖xa3 f3+ 33.♔e3 ♕g5+ 34.♔d3 ♖d8 35.♕d4 ♗e6

White resigned.

Scoring big
The pandemic and its impact on in-person chess tournaments is actually hurting the young guys the most, but it seems that Vincent Keymer didn't suffer that much. The young German GM had also played in the German Championship and Biel. After losing in the first round to Mickey Adams (Baden-Baden), Keymer (Deizisau) showed great resil-

ience and bounced back with a big score. In the process he also took down our (also my) Swiss friend.

NOTES BY
Vincent Keymer

**Noel Studer
Vincent Keymer**
Bundesliga 2020 (3)
Sicilian Defence, Najdorf Variation

As the pairings were only announced an hour before the start of the rounds, there was hardly any time to prepare. Nevertheless, this game saw a theoretical battle.

1.e4 A small surprise right away. I had counted on 1.d4.
1...c5 2.♘f3 d6 3.d4 cxd4 4.♘xd4 ♘f6 5.♘c3 a6 6.♗e3 e5 7.♘f3 ♗e7 8.♗c4 ♗e6

9.♗xe6 The critical try. White tries to punish the black move order in a concrete manner. 9.♗b3 leads to quieter positions.
9...fxe6 10.♘g5 ♕d7 11.♕f3

11...♘c6

11...d5!? would take the game into a completely different direction: 12.0-0-0 d4 13.♗xd4!? exd4 14.e5! 0-0! 15.♕h3 h6, with total chaos, but, as always, the verdict of the engine is 0.00 ☺
12.♕h3 ♘d8 13.♗b6 h6

14.0-0-0
Here, 14.♗xd8 ♖xd8 is fine for Black:
– 15.♕xe6+ ♕e7!? (perhaps the simplest solution) 16.♘d5 ♘xd5 17.♕g6+ ♔d7 18.♕f5+ ♔e8 19.♕g6+, with a draw.
– 15.0-0-0 ♗a5 16.f4! ♗xc3 17.bxc3 ♔e7! leads to unclear positions, but Black should have no problems.
– After 15.♘xe6 ♗a5 16.f4 exf4 17.0-0-0, 17...♗xc3! leads to an equal endgame by force: 18.bxc3 ♔f7 19.♘xf4 ♕xh3 20.♘xh3 ♘xe4 21.♖hf1+ ♔g6.
14...0-0 15.♗xd8 hxg5 16.♗xe7 ♕xe7 17.♕g3
17.♖d2 was the solid alternative.

17...b5! This was still preparation. It is very important not to allow White his play, but to create problems immediately. 17...g4?? 18.h3 is catastrophic for Black.
18.f3?!

After the game my opponent told me that he had mixed up the moves here. 18.f3 allows Black to solve all his problems without further ado and even to play for an advantage, whereas after 18.♕xg5 we would still be following the theory.

The main move is clearly 18.♕xg5, even though it leads to very unclear positions: 18...b4 19.♘e2 ♕c7! 20.f3 ♕c4 21.♕d2 d5!?, and here I will leave it to the reader to analyse this position further.

Germany's big hope Vincent Keymer continues to make impressive progress. Scoring 5½/7 the 15-year-old collected 20 rating points to reach a new Elo of 2608.

18...g4 This immediately solves all Black's problems. During the game I even had the feeling that Black's position was already more pleasant.

19.♖he1

A solid alternative for White was 19.a3 gxf3 20.gxf3 ♘h5, and this position should be about equal.

After 19.fxg4 b4 20.g5 bxc3 21.gxf6 cxb2+ 22.♔b1 ♖xf6 White has to fight for equality.

19...gxf3

An interesting alternative was 19...b4!? 20.♘a4 ♖ac8 21.fxg4 ♖c4 22.♕d3 ♖d4 23.♕xa6 ♘xg4 24.♖xd4 exd4, with compensation for the pawn.

20.♕xf3

Accepting a worse position.
20.gxf3 was a better choice: 20...b4 21.♘e2 a5 22.h4, when White has counterplay: 22...a4 23.♖g1, with chances for both sides.

20...♖ac8?! A standard move, which is a bit too timid here.
Clearly stronger was 20...b4! 21.♘a4 (21.♘e2 a5, and the black attack is too strong) 21...♖ac8 22.♔b1 ♕c7 23.♕b3 ♖fe8!, with a black edge.

21.♕d3

21.a3 would have used the chance to stabilize the position.

21...♖fd8

21...b4!? would have been stronger

here as well: 22.♘a4 (on 22.♘e2 Black plays 22...♕c6, followed by ...a5 and ...♖fc8, with a strong attack) 22...d5 23.exd5 exd5 24.♕xa6 ♕d7!, with more than enough compensation.

22.♔b1 ♖c4

23.a4!?

A big surprise. It looks quite illogical to weaken the king's position voluntarily, even though it will not be easy for Black to cover and protect everything. Safer was 23.a3.

23...♕e8 24.axb5?

White's only chance to somehow maintain equality was 24.g4! ♘xg4 25.♖g1 ♘f6 26.♕h3, with compensation for the pawn.

24...axb5 Things are looking bad for White. **25.b3**

25...♖c5 After the engine's suggestion 25...♖cc8!?, 26.g4! is White's best chance for counterplay: 26...b4 27.♘a4 d5 28.exd5 exd5 29.g5 ♘e4 30.♘e2 ♕c6 31.♖de1, and Black is better, but it's not so easy to make progress. Perhaps 31...♖d6!? is an option.
26.♘a2 Forced. **26...d5 27.exd5 ♘xd5!?** Strategically a catastrophe, but White has great difficulty parrying all the threats.

28.♕g3?! His best chance was the queen sac 28.♖xe5 ♘c3+ 29.♘xc3 ♖xd3 30.♖xc5 ♖xd1+ 31.♘xd1 ♕f8 32.♖c3! ♕f1 33.♔c1 ♕xg2 34.h3, when Black is clearly better, but White has good drawing chances.

28...♖dc8?
28...♕e7! leads to a forced win: 29.♖xe5 (here 29.♕xe5 won't work, as after 29...♘c3+ 30.♕xc3 ♖xc3 31.♘xc3 ♖a8 White cannot stabilize his position) 29...♕a7!, with the threat of ...♖a8. To avert this threat, White has to give up material, e.g. 30.♕g4 ♘c3+ 31.♘xc3 ♖xd1+ 32.♕xd1 ♖xe5, and Black wins.
29.♖xe5 ♖xc2 30.♖dxd5
This works for White. My opponent had very little time left, but nevertheless found the saving liquidation.
30...♕c6 31.♖d1 After 31.♘b4, 31...♖b2+! is a nice trick: 32.♔xb2 ♕c1+ 33.♔a2 ♖a8+ 34.♘a6 ♖xa6 mate.
31...♖xa2 32.♔xa2 ♕c2+ 33.♔a3 ♕xd1 34.♕e3!
White covers all important squares.

34...♕d6+ Unbelievable as it may seem, after 34...b4+ 35.♔xb4 ♖b8+ 36.♖b5 ♕g4+ 37.♔a5 ♖a8+ 38.♔b6 there is no way to exploit the weakness of the white king.
And after 34...♖a8+ 35.♔b4 the king is remarkably safe on b4.
35.♔b2 ♖a8 It may sound funny, but during the game I had the feeling that the white king would have been safer on b4 than on b2.
36.♖xe6 ♕a3+

37.♔c3?
Most certainly a mistake caused by time-trouble. After 37.♔c2! ♕a2+ 38.♔d3! ♕xb3+ 39.♔e2! White will save himself.
37...♖c8+ 38.♔d4 ♕b2+ 39.♔e4 ♕xg2+ 40.♔d4

Remarkably, there is no way to exploit the weak king's position immediately, but White will not survive the threats that will arise soon.
40...♕b2+
Only to reach the extra time after move 40.
41.♔d5 ♕g2+ 42.♔d4 ♕g4+ 43.♔d5 ♕d1+ 44.♔e5 ♕c2
This also wins, but 44...♖c2!? is probably even a bit more accurate.
45.♕h3
Since 45.♔f4 ♕xh2+ 46.♔g4 ♕g2+ 47.♔h4 ♖f8 is hopeless for White.
45...♖d8

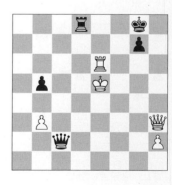

White is totally paralysed and cannot avoid heavy material losses.
46.♔f4 ♖d4+ 47.♔g5 ♖d5+ 48.♔f4 ♕f2+
And White resigned in view of 49.♔g4 ♕f5+ 50.♔g3 ♖d3+.

An inspired game

In Round 4, the classical clash between Baden-Baden and Solingen was on the menu. Since we did some good damage to them in the past, they always take us seriously, even though we had to make do without our top players this time. We always give them a hard time, and on this occasion it was no different. To begin with, Erwin l'Ami (Solingen) played an inspired game against world number two Fabiano Caruana (Baden-Baden).

NOTES BY
Erwin l'Ami

Erwin l'Ami
Fabiano Caruana
Bundesliga 2020 (4)
Queen's Gambit Declined

1.d4 ♘f6 2.c4 e6 3.♘f3 d5 4.♘c3 h6

This came as a small surprise, but I expected Fabiano Caruana to try and mix up the game one way or another, so in that sense a move like this was to be expected. Some months ago, I saw that Leela mentions this move as 'playable', but I did not analyse it seriously.

5.♗f4 ♗b4
The most ambitious move, fitting Caruana's intentions. Alternatively, 5...♗d6 6.♗xd6 ♕xd6 7.e3 gives White a small advantage and a very easy game.

6.cxd5 ♘xd5 7.♗d2 0-0

8.g3 At this point I was already looking at 8.g4, but I felt that 8...c5! would be a very effective rejoinder. Because of the speed with which my opponent was playing, I decided against 8.e4, which is obviously the critical move. After 8...♘xc3 9.bxc3 ♗a5, followed by ...c7-c5, the position is not so clear.

8...♘xc3 9.bxc3 ♗a5 10.g4
With the exchange on c3, the centre has stabilized somewhat, which made me think this move might be justified. I could have played 10.♗g2 c5 11.0-0, but in that case it is unlikely that I would be analysing this game for New In Chess magazine.

10...c5 The most natural move, and I was surprised to see that the computer suggests both 10...e5!? 11.♘xe5 c5, when Black has excellent compensation, and – even stronger – 10...♘c6!, with the idea of going ...e6-e5 next, regardless of what White does. This would have cast serious doubts on my 10th move.

11.♖g1 ♘c6
After the game Caruana mentioned 11...cxd4 12.cxd4 ♘c6, when 13.g5 hxg5 14.♖xg5 e5! was his point. And it's true that Black has excel-

lent compensation for the pawn after 15.dxe5 ♗e6.

12.dxc5

I was very happy with this move. Obviously, the idea is not to win a pawn, but to prevent Black from opening the centre with ...cxd4, which would have made the likelihood of a flank attack succeeding far more likely.

12...e5 13.♕c2
I spent some time on the line 13.g5 e4 14.gxh6 exf3 15.♖xg7+ ♔h8 16.♕c2 f5 17.0-0-0 ♕f6, but failed to find a follow-up. An engine check reveals that there probably isn't any. The text-move prepares castling queenside and makes a future g4-g5 push gain in strength.

13...♖e8
Only now does Black get into serious trouble. A very elegant solution was 13...e4! 14.♕xe4 ♖e8 15.♕c2 ♕d5, when Black has sacrificed another pawn to gain time. Here, 16.♗e3 ♖xe3 17.fxe3 ♕xc5 18.♔f2 ♗b6 19.♘d4 ♗d7 is a nice sample line, in which Black has great compensation. White should instead play 16.♘d4, with an open game.

14.g5 The logical follow-up, but not the best move. 14.0-0-0! is very strong, and now, after 14...e4 15.g5! exf3 (15...h5 16.g6! is an important point, as 16...exf3 17.gxf7+, followed by ♕g6+, is winning) 16.gxh6 f5 17.♖xg7+ ♔h8, 18.♗g5 is winning.

Erwin l'Ami: a moment to treasure, a fine victory against the world's number two.

14...g6
Instead, 14...hxg5! 15.♘xg5 e4 16.0-0-0 ♕d5 would have given Black excellent chances of putting up a successful defence. The endgame after 17.♕b3 ♕xb3 18.axb3 f6! is not clear, and 17.♖g3 ♕xc5 18.♗g2 ♗c7 19.♗xe4 ♗xg3 20.hxg3 is even less clear.

15.gxh6 e4 16.♘g5 ♗f5 17.0-0-0

While I liked the course that the game was taking at this point, it was by no means clear to me that my position was all that great. Objectively, I am already winning here, but the position is still messy, of course, especially in a practical game.

17...♕f6
After 17...e3, 18.♗xe3! ♗xc2 19.♖xd8 ♖axd8 20.♔xc2 is an exchange sacrifice I was very eager to make. The three extra pawns make it completely winning for White.

18.♗h3
An important one! White is happy to exchange the strong bishop on f5. 18...♗xh3 19.♘xh3 is followed by ♘h3-g5, with huge threats.

18...e3 19.♗xf5 exd2+ 20.♖xd2

20...♖e5
This caught me completely by surprise! I had been looking forward to 20...♕xf5 21.♕xf5 gxf5 22.h7+ ♔g7 23.♖d7 ♖e7 24.♘e4+! ♔h8 25.♘f6, and White wins. While this is good enough, much prettier is 23.h8♕+ ♖xh8 24.♘h7+!! ♔xh7 25.♖d3, and mate on h3.

21.♘xf7!
Not 21.e4 ♖xc5, and Black starts taking over the show on the queenside.

21...♕xf7 21...♖xf5 is met very strongly by 22.♘d6!, because after 22...♖g5 23.♖xg5 ♕xg5 24.♕b3+ the king doesn't have any good square to go to.
22.♗xg6 ♕xf2 Afterwards we discussed 22...♕f6 23.♖d6 ♕xf2 24.♗f7+ ♔h8 25.♕g6, which should also win. In fact, 23.♕b3+ ♔h8 24.♕xb7! wins on the spot.
23.♗f7+! The only move, but good enough! The g-file is decisively opened.
23...♔h8 There is nothing else. 23...♔xf7 24.♕h7+ is mate in a few moves, and after 23...♔f8 I had planned 24.♖g8+ ♔e7 25.h7.
24.♕g6 ♖g5

25.♖xg5 25.♕xg5 ♕xf7 26.♖d7 would have shortened the game considerably. **25...♗xc3 26.♔c2**

I thought this would clinch things. After the bishop moves, ♗g8 will lead to mate on h7.

26...♘e7

A bit of a shocker. I am obviously still completely winning, but with so little time this move was very unpleasant.

27.♕e4 ♗f6 28.♖e5 And here 28.e3 ♕f1 29.♗c4 ♕a1 30.♗d3! would have finished things instantly.

28...♖f8 29.e3 ♕f1 30.♗c4 ♕a1 31.♖xe7 ♕c3+

Another uncomfortable moment. I had miscalculated that after...

32.♔d1 ♕a1+ 33.♔c2 ♕c3+ 34.♔d1 ♕a1+ 35.♔e2 ♗xe7

... I couldn't recapture on e7 in view of the mating threat on f1.
Fortunately, the endgame that I am forced to liquidate into is still completely winning.

36.♕d4+ ♕xd4 37.exd4 ♖f4 38.♗d5

If b7 falls, the c- and d-pawns will decide easily.

38...♗f6 39.♔e3 ♖h4 40.♖d3

With move 40 reached, I got up from the board with a deep sense of relief. I had obviously not wrapped up the game in perfect fashion, but I was still

CHRISTIAN BOSSERT

Fabiano Caruana: one of the Baden-Baden stars happy to be back at the board again.

completely winning. Furthermore, the endgame is easy to convert.

40...♖h3+ 41.♔d2 ♖xh2+ 42.♔c3

42...♔h7

After the game, I proudly told Fabiano about the line 42...♖h5 43.♔c4 b5+ 44.♔xb5! ♖xd5 45.♔c6 ♖xd4 (or 45...♖d8 46.d5, and the passed pawns decide) 46.♖xd4 ♗xd4 47.♔d6, and White wins the endgame – upon which Fabiano observed that he hadn't played 42...♖h5 because of 43.♗f3, which is indeed winning instantly...

43.♗xb7 ♖xa2 44.♔b3 ♖a1 45.c6 ♗d8 46.d5

Unstoppable. The last thing to make sure of is that Black can't sacrifice his bishop for both passed pawns.

46...♗a5 47.d6 ♖c1 48.♖d5 ♗d8 49.♖d4

There is no stopping ♖c4, followed by c6-c7. Black resigned.

■ ■ ■

In the end, we lost convincingly, 6-2, one of the culprits being me myself. This is how I let Richard Rapport escape.

Loek van Wely
Richard Rapport
Bundesliga 2020 (4.1)
Queen's Gambit Declined, Baltic Defence

1.♘f3 d5 2.d4 ♗f5 3.c4 e6 4.♘c3 ♗b4

This is why it's so nice to play Richie. After four moves a totally new position has arisen (for me), and the

This is why it's so nice to play Richie. After four moves a totally new position has arisen (for me)

thing I mind least is thinking for myself.....
5.♕b3 ♘c6 6.♗g5 ♘ge7 7.e3 a5 8.a3 a4 9.♕d1 ♗xc3+ 10.bxc3 f6 11.♗f4 ♕d7 12.♘h4 ♗e4 13.f3 ♗g6 14.♘xg6 hxg6 15.♖b1 b6 16.♕c2 ♔f7

This was an interesting moment from a strategic point of view. I thought for quite some time, but unfortunately I couldn't come up with the right solution.
17.♗d3

Better was the prophylactic 17.♗g3 or 17.♔f2.
17...dxc4 18.♗xc4 ♘d5 19.♗xd5
A sad necessity. After 19.0-0 Black has 19...g5.
19...exd5 20.c4 g5 21.♗g3 ♖he8 22.♔f2

22...f5? Better was 22...♕e6 23.♕c3 ♘e7! 24.♖he1, and although I prefer White, Black also has chances. The comp tells Black to give up a pawn: 24...c5 25.dxc5 bxc5 26.cxd5 ♘xd5 27.♕xc5 ♖ac8 28.♕d4 ♖c2+ 29.♔g1

♘c3 30.♕d3 ♕a2 31.♖b7+ ♖e7 32.♖xe7+ ♔xe7 33.♔h1, with some vague business that Richie would have loved.
23.cxd5 ♕xd5 24.♖hc1 ♖e6

25.♕c4?? Played without thinking, which explains the double question mark. After 25.♗xc7 Black is toast.
25...♘e7 White still looks completely in control. How to get mated on the h-file in six moves? With the help of Richie I managed!
26.♖b5 c5 27.dxc5

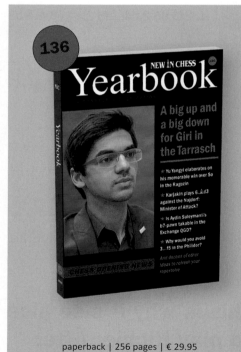

27.♕xd5 would have been safer.
27...♕d2+

And although I saw Black's next move coming, I nevertheless played:
28.♔f1? 28.♔g1 was still good.
28...♘d5 29.♗f2 ♖h8

Of course I didn't see this one coming, and once you start missing moves and seeing ghosts, the end is very near.
30.♔g1?? After 30.h3 I would be worried about 30...g4, of course. One way to escape was 30.c6: 30...♖xh2 31.♖xd5 ♖h1+ 32.♗g1 ♕xe3 33.♖d7+ ♔g6 34.♕xe6+ ♕xe6 35.♖d3. And best was 30.♕c2.
30...♘xe3 31.♕c3 ♖xh2

And oops. White resigned.

The big clash

The championship saw its culmination in Round 7 with the big clash that we had all been waiting for between Baden-Baden and Viernheim, with Baden-Baden having draw odds because they were ahead in board points. Their stars were scoring really well: Vachier-Lagrave 4 from 5; Mickey Adams 6/7; Paco Vallejo 5½/6; and Arkadij Naiditsch 5½/6.

Although Etienne Bacrot lost to Sergey Fedorchuk on the last board (8), Vallejo and Naiditsch decided the issue on Boards 6 and 7. Vallejo managed to catch a queen in broad daylight.

Bassem Amin
Paco Vallejo
Bundesliga 2020 (7)

position after 16.♕xe5

Not much is going on here and the position is more or less equal. Bassem Amin, not known for out-preparing his opponents, but for outplaying them, logically continues the fight, but surprisingly gets into trouble very fast.

Paco Vallejo won a queen in broad daylight.

16...♘g4 17.♕f4 ♘f6 18.♕e5 ♘g4 19.♕d4 ♘f6 20.cxd5 e5 21.♕c5 cxd5 22.♕b5?
Not sensing the danger!

22...♖e6! 23.♖c2??
Blunders never come alone. With a nice sequence Black is now going to trap White's queen.
23...♖b6 24.♕a4 ♗f5!

Germany Bundesliga 2020		
	MP	BP
1 OSG Baden-Baden	14	43-13
2 SC Viernheim	12	38-18
3 SF Deizisau	10	33-23
4 SV Werder Bremen	8	29-27
5 SG Solingen	6	27½-28½
6 FC Bayern München	4	23½-32½
7 Schachfreunde Berlin	1	16½-39½
8 Aachener SV 1856	1	13½-42½

25.♖c5

If 25.♕h4 then 25...g5 26.♕xh6 ♘g4 27.♕h5 ♖h6 traps the queen.
25...♗d7 26.♕h4 g5 27.♕xh6 ♘e4

Forcing Bassem to give up his queen for a rook and a few pawns, which wasn't enough of course.
28.♕xb6 ♕xb6 29.♘xe4 dxe4 30.♖xe5 exd3 31.♖xg5+ ♔f8 32.exd3 ♖c8
And Black won easily (0-1, 41).

In his game against Igor Kovalenko, Arkadij Naiditsch didn't miss his chance when he could grab the initiative early on.

Arkadij Naiditsch
Igor Kovalenko
Bundesliga 2020 (7)

position after 9.♖e1

First of all some nice words for my friend Arkadij. Although he has been the subject of a lot of Schadenfreude, I do admire him. He is absolutely a great fighter. But unfortunately for him, a lot depends on his confidence level. When confident, he beats Magnus like it's another day at the office, but without confidence, the guy becomes more than mortal, a sitting duck (albeit still with a big mouth!). When our team of Solingen play against Baden-Baden, we are always happy to see both Arkadij and Richard (Rapport). Arkadij is known for winning matches, but also for losing them! And since we are always the underdogs, Arkadij and Richie are our only hopes ☺. From this game I would like to highlight this fragment, because I believe that at this point, the game has already been decided in a higher sense.

When I saw this position my first idea was 9...♗e4, in order to stop d5, but then Kovalenko went:
9...♕c8 And then I thought, well, interesting! But then Arkadij went:
10.♕c2 And I thought, hmm.
10...♗e4
And when he went: **11.♕b3**

Backing down and leaving the initiative to Arkadij. I can tell you, a very bad idea

Handing Arkadij Naiditsch the initiative, a very bad idea.

MICHAEL ZAHN

I thought: Wait, isn't this running into ...♘c6-a5, with tempo??
11...d6 12.♗f1 ♘c6 13.♗g5 ♘a5 14.♕d1

14...♘d7??

Backing down and leaving the initiative to Arkadij. I can tell you, a very bad idea. Although it still got a bit tricky later, I don't think the result was ever really in doubt anymore. 14...♘xc4 would have been the logical consequence of what had gone before, and only god knows what would have happened.
15.♘d2 ♗g6 16.e4

With a serious advantage for White, who went on to win (1-0, 69). ∎

Elon Musk: 'Tesla is best understood as a collection of about a dozen startups, mostly in series, increasingly in parallel. Every product line [and] new production system was invented. So instead of playing chess with the same pieces as everyone else, create new pieces.' *(The billionaire tech entrepreneur, on the key to Tesla's research and development prowess)*

Marina Hyde: 'Boris Johnson's government is surrounded by enablers of its delusions, from imbecilic Tory MPs to panting journalists who still reckon it's all some brilliant game of 4D chess.' *(The Guardian columnist on the UK government's handling of Brexit and the pandemic)*

A.A. Milne: 'It is impossible to win gracefully at chess. No man has yet said "Mate!" in a voice which failed to sound to his opponent bitter, boastful and malicious.' *(The chess-loving author of Winnie The Pooh)*

Jay Rosen: 'The deep grammar is still symmetrical: Biden is doing this, Trump is doing that. As if there's a chessboard between them. This is a distortion. There is one normal candidacy competing against an attempt to trigger a national emergency and crash the system.' *(The US writer and professor of journalism at New York University, on the media coverage battle lines of the unfolding US Presidential election)*

Jeremy Silman: 'The best move isn't the best move if you don't know why it is best.' *(In his acclaimed book, How To Reassess Your Chess)*

H.G. Wells: 'The passion for playing chess is one of the most unaccountable in the world. It slaps the theory of natural selection in the face. It is the most absorbing of occupations. The least satisfying of desires. A nameless excrescence upon life.'

Boris Spassky: 'Probably my time at university was not very useful, and I lost five years. Fischer may be right when he says that it is a bad idea for a chess master to study hard at school or university.' *(In an interview with Leonard Barden for Chess Life & Review, shortly after becoming world champion in 1969)*

Carla Berkowitz: 'The image and story was haunting and I felt like I had a quantum shift in my perception of chess and who plays it.' *(The producer of the new chess-themed hit movie Critical Thinking based on the true story of the inner-city Miami-Jackson High chess team)*

Dr Norman Reider: 'Not without reason is it the one game that, since its invention around A.D. 600, has been played in most of the world, has captivated the imagination and interest of millions, and has been the source of great sorrows and great pleasures.' *(In his 1959 paper*

Chess, Oedipus, and the Mater Dolorosa in The International Journal of Psychoanalysis)

Tigran Petrosian: 'The chess public sees the grandmasters as if in an oblique mirror. So I am considered to be too cautious, while in fact I try only to avoid danger.' *(At the opening press conference for the 1970 USSR v Rest of the World Match in Belgrade)*

Miguel Najdorf: 'I do not believe the Soviet players are more talented than the others. They are just more inclined to consider chess work rather than play.' *(At that same press conference)*

Alexander Grischuk: 'I don't see any drawbacks in Fischer Random chess. The only slight shortcoming is the start position, otherwise there are just advantages.' *(Said during the recent St Louis Chess 9XL)*

Viktors Pupols: 'No matter what else happens in life, you can sit down to a chess board and you will always find the same number of ranks and files; there is always a white square in the right corner and if you make the moves, you will do well. In life, you could make all the right decisions and still wind up in the streets.' *(The 86-year-old four-time Washington State Champion, who once famously beat the young Bobby Fischer with the Latvian Gambit)*

Judit Polgar

Ivanchuk's lessons

Few players can be so deeply and beautifully lost in thought as Vasyl Ivanchuk. And when the Ukrainian legend withdraws to 'Planet Chuky', his opponents know that the Force is against them. **JUDIT POLGAR** has known Ivanchuk from an early age and tells us what she has learnt from him.

Caissa is a demanding goddess, and those touched by her charms can never completely free themselves from her chains of passion. There are a few chosen ones, though, who seem to dedicate every single thought and breath to fathoming her deepest secrets. I cannot think of a better example of this kind of voluntary slavery than Vasyl Ivanchuk.

I first met him when I was 12, at the Lucerne 1989 World Teams. Ukraine was still part of the Soviet Union and Vasyl, 20 at the time, still went by the name Vassily. He had missed a win against the almighty Kasparov earlier in the tournament, and the game kept haunting him. He took the first opportunity that presented itself to show the critical position to me and my sister Susan, explaining all the tiny analytical and psychological details.

We met again in New York later that year, and I was amazed that he

spent hours playing blitz with me and other players weaker than him. He took every game as a challenge and an opportunity to create instant puzzles for his ever-curious mind. It is small wonder that Vasyl maintains a high level of chess in rapid and blitz games.

The following episode from one of the Amber Rapid and Blindfold tournaments in Monaco is indicative of Ivanchuk's permanent focus on chess in general, and on his own games in particular. According to the schedule, we played four games a day, with relatively long breaks between them. Most of the players, including myself, used this time to relax and freshen up in our hotel rooms. When returning for the next game, I more than once noticed that Ivanchuk had not moved from where I had seen him when I left, clearly absorbed in his previous game.

Ivanchuk has a universal style, but I can identify a few important trademarks.

Trademark 1 – the ability to grasp the essence of the position. There are several levels of understanding and assessing a position. Typically, the absolute truth is hiding under a few layers of superficial evidence, but Vasyl usually evinces the necessary depth. Here is an example.

Vasyl Ivanchuk
Judit Polgar
Monaco Amber blindfold 1995

position after 20...♖be8

Both sides are optimally mobilized, with one exception: my queen's knight is passive and requires a big effort to activate. I was relying on the fact that the position is blocked, and exerted pressure on f4, inhibiting the

There are a few chosen ones, who seem to dedicate every single thought and breath to fathoming Caissa's deepest secrets

Vasyl Ivanchuk: a universal player with a unique passion for the game.

Vasyl Ivanchuk
Judit Polgar
Cap d'Agde rapid 2010

position after 13...♕c7

White has a considerable advance in development, but I thought that his king's presence in the centre would offer me counterplay. Ivanchuk found a courageous and creative way to prove me wrong.

14.♕a3! Keeping my king in the centre and threatening ♘d6+.

14...♕f4+ In connection with the next move, the best practical chance.

15.♔e2 d5 16.g3!

Forcing my queen to abandon control of d6, because after 16.♘d6+ ♔d7 White would be hanging a bit: 17.exd5 (the point of the check on f4 is that White cannot consolidate with 17.e5 in view of to 17...♘xd4+, and wins) 17...exd5 18.♘f5 ♔c7 19.♘e3 (19.♘xg7 ♗g4 yields me a winning counterattack) 19...♖e8, with excellent counterplay.

16...♕g4 17.♘d6+ ♔d7

The threat ...♘xd4+ looks hard to meet, but Ivanchuk had calculated everything.

18.♔e3!!

---

only constructive pawn break. After White's next move, however, this proved to be a superficial truth.

21.f4! This not only creates pressure in the centre, but also obstructs the c1-h6 diagonal, making ♘f5 a threat.

21...exf4 21...♘b7 could also be met by 22.♘f5.

22.♘f5! ♗xf5 One of the points behind White's 21st move is that after 22...gxf5? 23.♕xh5 the knight on d2 is not hanging.

23.exf5 ♕d8 24.♘e4 The position has opened and White is attacking with an extra piece.

24...♗g7 25.♗xg7 ♘xg7 26.♕a1 f6 27.fxg6 hxg6 28.gxf4 ♘b7

29.f5!? The most energetic continuation, maintaining White's initiative,

while I am struggling to recycle my knight.

29...gxf5 29...♘xf5? weakens the defence of the rook on e8, allowing 30.♘xf6+!, winning.

30.♘g3 ♖e5 31.♗h3 ♕e8

32.♘xf5? 32.♗xf5! would have preserved White's advantage.

32...♕h5 Suddenly, White's pieces are hanging. **33.♘e7+ ♔f7 34.♘c6 ♕xh3 35.♘xe5+ dxe5 36.♕xe5 ♔g6** At this point, the position is unclear, and the game ended in a draw on move 59.

Closely related to the previous one is **Trademark 2 – the courage to implement principled plans, no matter how paradoxical**.

The king bravely steps forward, defending everything and creating the threats 19.exd5 (19...exd5 20.♗f5+) and 19.♘xf7, amongst others.

18...f5
My last attempt at counterplay, elegantly parried by Ivanchuk.

19.♗e2!
Suddenly, my queen is in trouble.

19...fxe4

20.h3! A clear sign of maximalism. Ivanchuk intends to win the queen under the most favourable circumstances. 20.♘e5+ should have won, too, but Vasyl did not wish to allow me to activate my minor pieces with 20...♘gxe5 21.♗xg4 ♘xg4+ 22.♔d2.

20...♕xf3+ There is nothing better, because after 20...♕h5 21.♘e5+ White wins the queen for just a knight.

21.♗xf3 exf3 22.♖hc1
And White won (1-0, 57).

I find the sequence between moves 14 and 20 impressive. With the possible exception of 20.h3, Ivanchuk's moves were the only ones leading to a clear win, even though it may have looked as if they offered me dangerous counterplay.

Trademark 3 – tactical sharpness.
I owe a great part of my successes to my ability to deliver tactical tricks at critical junctions or turning points. This used to be especially effective in blitz games, but in the next game it backfired painfully, which suggests that Ivanchuk was outstandingly sharp at this speed, too.

Vasyl Ivanchuk
Judit Polgar
Moscow WC blitz 2009

position after 28.♖e1

White has an extra pawn and the bishop pair, and my control in the centre hardly compensates for them. In my search for saving chances, I spotted a small trick.

28...♗h6 29.♕d1 ♕c6!? 30.♗xf7 ♕c2!?

This is the position I had pinned some hopes on. White cannot capture any of my major pieces, since this would allow an intermediate back rank check. Furthermore, I am threatening ...♘e2+, followed by ...♘xg3, and my overall activity seems to offer me some chances.

31.♗xg6+! But no longer, after this little combination!
After 31...♔xg6, 32.♕xc2 pins and wins the rook. 1-0.

There were times when many considered a world title match between Kasparov and Ivanchuk imminent, but Vasyl never made it to Challenger. A possible reason was that, absorbed

Absorbed in his usual deep thoughts, Ivanchuk sometimes overlooked very simple things

in his usual deep thoughts, he sometimes overlooked very simple things. Here is an anecdotal episode.

Vasyl Ivanchuk
Judit Polgar
Mexico City rapid 2010

position after 93...♖e4-f4

I had had the initiative for a long time, including a clear win at some point, but then I allowed things to spin out of control, and my last move, 93...♖e4-f4, was an out-and-out blunder... Ivanchuk missed 94.♕h3, mate, and after another mistake on his part on move 113(!), my last remaining pawn decided the game.

Conclusions
■ When designing a plan, one should try to look beyond the superficial elements of the position in search of the essential truth.
■ In double-edged fights, it is important to display the courage to play the most principled moves, despite the apparent risks involved.
■ One should develop one's tactical sharpness in order to be able to crown one's superior strategy in the critical moments.
■ Never allow (or miss) a mate in one! ■

1. Korchmar-Vetokhin
chess.com 2020

16.♘g6+! ♞xg6 **17.♖xh7+!** Black resigned in view of 17...♚xh7 18.♛h5 mate.

2. Sadhwani-Mikhalevski
lichess.org 2020

37.♖xh6+! ♚xh6 **38.♛h2+!** They say backward moves are often overlooked. Black resigned in view of 38...♚g6 39.♛h5 mate.

3. Dubov-Ivanisevic
chess.com 2020

31.♖c8+! ♞f8 Black can't take as the queen hangs on a7. **32.♖xf8+!** Black resigned since after the other capture 32...♚xf8, 33.♛h8 is mate.

4. Pasti-Budisavljevic
Paracin 2020

37...♞c4+ Not going for exchanges, but with something completely different in mind: **38.♞xc4 ♗xf4+!** White resigned. He has to give up the queen to avoid the wonderful mate 39.♚xf4 ♛f2.

5. Warmerdam-Leenhouts
lichess.org 2020

White started a forced sequence where he had to foresee a nice shot on the fourth move: **17.♗g6+!** hxg6 **18.♛xg6+ ♚e7 19.♗c5+ ♚e6 20.♞d4+! exd4 21.♖ae1** Mate.

6. Sivuk-Sydoryka
Kiev 2020

30.♗xg5! hxg5 31.♛h4+! 31.♖xg5 ♖c1+ 32.♚h2 ♖h1+! 33.♚g3! ♛c3+ 34.♖d3 ♛e1+ 35.♛xe1 ♖xe1 36.♖d4 ♗f5! is not mate yet. **31...♚g7 32.♖xg5+ ♚f8 33.♛h8+** and Black got mated soon.

7. Kobalia-Xiong
lichess.org 2020

35.♗xh6! ♚g8 If 35...♖xh6 36.♛xf7+ ♚h8 37.♛g7 mate. **36.♛xg6+!** An excellent and indispensable follow-up. **36...fxg6 37.f7+** Black resigned as after 37...♚xf7 (37...♚h7 38.f8♛) 38.♞d6+ he'll be an exchange down.

8. Georgiev-Stojanovic
Tivat 2011

27.♞g4! ♛xf4 28.♞xf6+ ♛xf6 28...gxf6 loses to 29.♛h7+ ♚f8 30.♖xe7! ♗e6 31.♖1xe6! ♛c1+ 32.♖e1. **29.♛h7+ ♚f8 30.♛h8+** 30.♖xe7? g5! throws away the win. **30...♞g8 31.♛xg8+! ♚xg8 32.♖xe8+ ♖xe8 33.♖xe8** Mate.

9. Yakubboev-Tristan
chess.com 2020

21.♖xd4! ♖xd4 22.♞c5 b6 22...♚d8 23.♛xb7 gives no escape for the king. **23.♖e8+ ♖d8 24.♛d5!** A devastating blow. Facing a tough choice between 24...bxc5 25.♖xd8 mate and 24...♖xe8 25.♛a8 mate, Black resigned.

Letter from Lockdown

During the pandemic our sense of time is changing and who knows what else. **MATTHEW SADLER** even wonders if chess books are getting bigger! The new games collections of David Navara and Tigran Petrosian are certainly hefty tomes, but he also reviews less heavy works. Such as Keith Arkell's book on endings that reminded him of Capablanca's *Chess Fundamentals*.

As the Covid-19 lockdown in the UK enters its sixth month (with Brexit as a nice UK-specific bonus) it's fair to say that I'm in a state of perpetual confusion. Once this is over, I think my enduring memory of this time will be of scratching my head when hearing the latest government advice and thinking 'Isn't this the opposite to what they said yesterday?' and 'I'd never thought I'd hear a government minister say that'!

It may just be a sign of age and lack of flexibility, because I have similar feelings of confusion in chess after a steady diet of blitz and rapid events. Don't get me wrong – it's wonderful that chess has achieved so much exposure online and the drama of some of these events has been

amazing. However, I was shocked to realise that I can barely remember any of the moves of the games I had watched, which is not something I'm used to! It adds to the general feeling of not quite knowing what has happened with the time I've spent in lockdown. It's also typical of these topsy-turvy times that I've been getting my necessary fix of slow chess at classical time controls by watching the superhuman engines at the TCEC chess engine championship! And finally, I looked at my table, on which I'd placed the books to review for the coming months and I thought: 'Is it me or are chess books getting bigger?'

My Chess World by David Navara (Thinkers Publishing) certainly fits that description, with over 600 pages

of mind-bogglingly complex games! The book is an updated combination of two of Navara's Czech-language books. These books themselves were partly derived from blog articles that Navara wrote for the Prague Chess Society from about 2009. The book is a collection of 64 games, organised chronologically, starting in 2001 and ending in 2019.

At regular intervals between games, Navara spends a few pages describing his life at that period, his chess form, and the background to the events he competed in. Navara has an engaging writing style, open about likes and dislikes and with a self-deprecating sense of humour. A nice example is when he talks about the value of sport for chess players (he isn't a fan!): 'Are you interested to know the best sports for chess players? I believe they are horse-racing, boxing, swimming, and running. The reasoning behind *horse-racing* is evident – one should be able to lead his/her steeds and demonstrate their abilities. *Boxing* belongs here because it improves the ability to strike and combine attack with defence. Moreover, several tournaments use the knockout system, and the hybrid sport of chess boxing has become quite popular recently. The importance of *swimming* is related to the ability to control the flow of the game as well as to deep calculation. It's no coincidence that the chess programs Rybka (little fish) and Stockfish excel in this regard! But *running* is the key one, mainly due to the increased use of the zero-tolerance rule. When arriving late means losing by default, the connection between physical condition and results at the board is self-evident.'

His selection of games demonstrates this same modesty, as Navara also annotates quite a few losses and draws. Navara is one of a few dozen players just under the world elite and a relatively small number of his games is widely known to

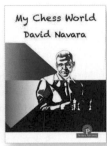

**My Chess World
David Navara
Thinkers Publishing
2020**
★★★★☆

the average chess fan (his amazing king march to h8 in a 6.♗e3 Najdorf Sicilian against Wojtaszek at Biel 2015 is one example), which makes this a rewarding book to read through, full of great chess that you'd never seen before! His (sometimes excessively) active style has produced many exciting games and all the games in this book are extremely entertaining. The annotations are very thorough so I can't present a whole game to you, but I'll just take this extract which had me oohing and aahing as I read through it. We join the game as Navara has played the sharp 29.♖d7.

**David Navara
Robert Kempinski**
Gorzow Wielkopolski 2014

position after 29.♖d7?

29...♖xc2!!

'I had seen this sacrifice but missed Black's thirty-second move. GM

Kempinski deserves the highest credit, as he played this part of the game very well despite his time-trouble!'

30.♖xb7

'The h4-pawn would decide the game in Black's favour after 30.♗xf6? ♕xd7! 31.♖xc2 ♖xc2.'

30...♖c1+ 31.♔a2 ♗xe5 32.♖b2

'White should avoid 32.♖d1? ♖8c2+ 33.♕xc2 ♖xc2+ 34.♔b1 ♖xf2, and especially 32.♖xg7+?? ♔xg7 33.♖d7+ ♔h8 34.♖xh7+ ♔xh7 35.♕h5+ ♔g8 36.♕xe5 ♖8c2+.'

32...h3!

'Quite an unpleasant surprise, as I had expected 32...♗xb2. The position deserves a diagram. Black only has a bishop and pawn for his queen, but what a bishop and what a pawn! Black is threatening ...h2, winning! I decided to first find a way to draw and then search for a win. While the latter objective is unattainable, even the former was far from easy. I found the right idea at the last minute and its correct implementation at the very last moment. Playing 29.♖d7? I had the line 32...♗xb2? 33.♔xb2 h3 34.♖b8!! in mind. Sometimes it is better to see less. Here it might have prevented me from making a mistake on move twenty-nine.'

33.♕h5!

'I was down to nine seconds before

getting a 30-second increment. A move or two later I even went down to a couple of seconds. The perils awaiting White are aptly illustrated by the following line: 33.f4 ♗xb2 34.♕xb2 ♖8c2 35.♖xg7+ ♔h8 36.♖g2+ ♔xb2+ 37.♔xb2 ♖g1, when Black is winning after ...♖g2. While 33.♖d7 ♗xb2 34.♔xb2 h2 35.♖d1 h1♕ 36.♖xh1 ♖xh1 might be objectively equal, White needs to pay attention.'

33...♗xb2 34.♖e7 h6 35.e5!

'White should avoid 35.♖e8+ ♖xe8 36.♕xe8+ ♔h7 37.♔xb2 (White can maintain equality after 37.♕h5 ♗d4 38.b4 ♖c3 but should avoid this line as it is extremely dangerous. Black plays 39...g6, puts his bishop on g7 and tries to support his h3-pawn with his rook) 37...h2, when Black is better thanks to his safer king.'

35...♗xe5

'The bishop is untouchable because of 38...♖8c2+. The engines show that 35...♔h7/h8 was also enough for a draw.'

36.♖e8+ ♖xe8 37.♕xe8+ ♔h7 38.♕xe5 ♖c2+ 39.♔b1

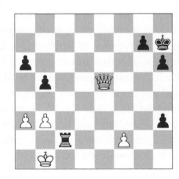

39...♖xf2

'Black's pawn is about to enter the second rank, if not the first. It is time to force a draw.'

40.♕e4+ ♔h8 41.♕e8+ ♔h7 42.♕e4+ ½-½

'I naturally played for a win, but I still liked the game quite a lot and so did many other players. I love chess due to such games. I was less enthusiastic about the match result (2-4), but losses are also part of the game. Alas,

Navara's (sometimes excessively) active style has produced many exciting games and all the games in this book are extremely entertaining

at the end of the season my team lacked the half point necessary for first place.'

A really good book, warmly recommended! 4 stars!

■ ■ ■

Petrosian Year by Year, Volume I (1942-1962) by Tibor Karolyi and Tigran Gyozalyan (Elk and Ruby) is the first of a two-volume set dealing with the life and games of the great Armenian. This volume of nearly 500 pages starts in 1942, with a simultaneous game against Salo Flohr played when Petrosian was just 13, and takes us through chronologically to the Varna Olympiad of 1962, when Petrosian was already established as one of the world's best players. There is a foreword by Levon Aronian and a selection of rare photos from this period.

Although many of Petrosian's games are well-known, those are mostly games from his period as World Champion. I had given many of the games in this book no more than a cursory glance so it's always refreshing to see such games analysed in detail and to have the interesting points you may have missed pointed out to you. The annotations are generally fairly light and easy to read without a board but there are a few passages of extremely deep analysis. The famous rook ending between Petrosian and Fischer at the Portoroz Interzonal 1958 is analysed exhaustively,

**Petrosian Year by Year
Volume I (1942-1962)
Tibor Karolyi & Tigran
Gyozalyan
Elk and Ruby, 2020**
★★★★☆

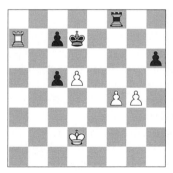

Petrosian-Fischer
Portoroz 1958 (13)
position after 52...♔xd7

while GM Ferenc Berkes does some sterling work on a bishop and extra pawn vs knight ending with all the pawns on the same side that could have arisen in Petrosian's game with Tal in the first round of the 1962 Curaçao Candidates Tournament (from which Tal later had to withdraw) as well as the rook ending that actually did arise:

Petrosian-Tal
Curaçao 1962 (1)
position after 42.h3

I enjoyed the book greatly. The only thing that appealed to me a little less is a consequence of the authors' desire to be as exhaustively complete as possible. Every round of each tournament is described briefly up to the point an annotated game from a specific round is presented. This can sometimes run to a whole page of text that at some point caused my eyes to glaze over a little. Some little diagrams might have helped to alleviate that problem. However, this is a minor quibble on an otherwise excellently produced book. I'm looking forward very much to seeing the second volume! 4 stars!

■ ■ ■

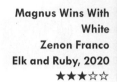

**Magnus Wins With
White
Zenon Franco
Elk and Ruby, 2020**
★★★☆☆

Magnus Wins With White by Zenon Franco (Elk and Ruby) is another 2-part series (*Magnus Wins With Black* will follow shortly). Thirty-two games won by Magnus Carlsen with White between 2004 and 2020 are annotated in a question-and-answer style. The book is adorned with a foreword by Magnus Carlsen's chief second Peter Heine Nielsen.

Not long ago, I reviewed an excellent book by Franco on Emanuel Lasker and it's interesting to note how many similarities Franco sees between Carlsen and Lasker: 'Considering their high level of play, neither of them attached much importance to the opening (even though there are several variations named after Lasker). Rather they were extremely gifted in both the middlegame and the ending and possessed the capacity to play for a win to the very end. Lasker has probably won more games than any other world champion from

It's interesting to note how many similarities Franco sees between Carlsen and Lasker

positions that were objectively lost or "dead drawn". Carlsen wins more equal endings or those predicted to be a draw, but he has also posted several "Laskerian" examples.'

The annotations are not too heavy, which makes them pleasant to read without the use of a board. One innovation is a little list after each game entitled 'Some lessons from this game'. I like the idea, but I had mixed feelings about the execution, as those notes often seemed on the terse side to me. The games are well-chosen, albeit inevitably extremely familiar, and reflect the staggering versatility of the world's best player, both in terms of openings and types of positions. All-in-all, an enjoyable book, 3 stars!

■ ■ ■

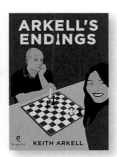

Arkell's Endings
Keith Arkell
Ginger GM, 2020
★★★☆☆

Arkell's Endings by Keith Arkell is a first publication by GingerGM aka GM Simon Williams, best known until now for a successful series of DVDs such as *Killer French* and *Killer Dutch*! The English grandmaster Keith Arkell has been a regular and popular presence on the English weekend circuit for as long as I can remember (and maybe he can too!) and his style is honed for winning large numbers of games with a minimal amount of complications. Keith was an ideal candidate to feature in the book Natasha Regan and I co-wrote called *Chess for Life*, as he had used more or less the same opening repertoire throughout his career and not only managed to maintain his level of play but even to increase it as he got older.

A great deal of Keith's success is based on an excellent practical endgame technique. We featured Keith's handling of rook endings in *Chess for Life* and indeed Keith has won more same-side rook and 4 pawns vs rook and 3 pawns endings (and 3 vs 2, and 2 vs 1, and 1 vs 0...) than any other player in the UK! In 160 pages, *Arkell's Endings* features a selection of 33 endings, each with an explicitly practical character. The annotations are also of a very practical character, focusing little on variations and much more on the feeling that Keith had while playing the game. It's an unusual book in the modern era – it made me think of Capablanca's *Chess Fundamentals* while I was reading it! – but extremely readable and instructive.

Let me show you an extract from

a game in a typical Caro-Kann pawn structure that Keith has played all his life and handles extremely well.

Pavel Certek
Keith Arkell
Vienna 2016
French Defence, Tarrasch Variation

1.d4 e6 2.e4 d5 3.♘d2 c5 4.exd5 ♕xd5 5.♘gf3 cxd4 6.♗c4 ♕d6 7.0-0 ♘f6 8.♘b3 ♘c6 9.♘bxd4 ♘xd4 10.♕xd4 ♕xd4 11.♘xd4 a6 12.♖e1 ♗c5 13.♘b3 ♗d6 14.♗e3 ♘g4 15.g3 ♘xe3 16.♖xe3 ♔e7

'I've learnt by now that to win such positions requires a lot of grinding. Small advantages will have to be accumulated in the hope that at some point White's position will become critical and then indefensible.'

17.♗f1 ♖d8 18.♗g2 ♗c7 19.c4 a5
'I could have spent any amount of time choosing between this move and the more restrained but equally

It's an unusual book in the modern era – it made me think of Capablanca's *Chess Fundamentals*

good 19...♖b8. When there is little to analyse by way of concrete variations, I like to make quick decisions, saving my time and energy for later on.'
20.♖e2 a4 21.♘c5 ♖a7 22.♖c1 ♗b6 23.♘e4 ♗d4 24.♔f1 ♖a5

'This is my problem piece and I'm looking for a way to give it more scope, whereas my light-squared bishop can sit happily on c8 for the time being. Since it isn't easy to coordinate the rooks it will probably suit me to exchange one of them at some point and then carefully expand on the kingside.'
25.♘c3 ♗c5 26.f4 ♔f8 27.♔e1 h6 28.♖d2 ♖xd2 29.♔xd2 g5
'A dual-purpose move. I am trying to create weaknesses in my opponent's structure and at the same time clear the way for the e- and f-pawns.'
30.♖f1 ♗e7 31.♔d3 a3
'Played reluctantly. I would have preferred to leave this pawn on a4, or even better a5, to keep White's queenside pawns in check, but I wanted to free up my rook for active duty.'
32.b3 gxf4 33.♖xf4 ♖h5

'This is perhaps the most important moment of the game. If I can induce

White to play h2-h4, then not only will his pawns become weaker, but he will lose the option of playing h2-h3 and g3-g4 to try and break up the centre which I later intend to erect.'

34.h4 ♖e5 35.♖e4 ♖f5 36.♖e3 b6 37.♖f3 ♖e5 38.♖e3 ♖f5 39.♖f3 ♖h5 40.♖e3 ♗c5 41.♖e2 ♖f5 42.♘e4 ♗e7 43.♔c3 ♖e5 44.♔d4 f6

'You may wonder why I am taking so much time to mobilise my pawns, but it has been known since the days of Steinitz and Tarrasch that to get the most out of the bishop pair, you should take central squares away from the opposing knight. Hence it would be a gross positional error to move the pawn from e6 and cede the d5-square at this point. Eventually the e- and f-pawns will need to get moving, but patience is required.'

45.♘c3 ♗d6 46.♔d3 ♖xe2

'That's enough pottering around. It's now time for my two bishops to flex their muscles.'

47.♘xe2 f5 48.♔c3 ♗d7

'Finally I move this piece – for the first time. Unlike knights, bishops can often do a perfectly good job from the back rank. The intention is to discourage 49.b4 on account of the annoying reply 49...♗a4, which prevents ♔b3 and threatens ...♗d1.'

49.♗f3 e5 50.♔d2 ♗b4+ 51.♔d1 ♔e7

'Inch by inch my position has become very nice. I can use my flexible pawns to continue gaining space and continue pushing him back.'

52.♔c2 ♔d6 53.♗h5 ♗c6 54.♘c3 ♔c5 55.g4

'As so often happens, rather than sit tight and watch his position slowly deteriorate, Certek lashes out, missing a tactic in the process.'

55...♗f3 56.♘a4+

'I expected 56.♘d5 but was sure there would be more than one way to win. Had he played this, I would have had to settle down and, for the first time in the game, do some calculating.'

56...♔d4 57.♘xb6 fxg4

'Material is still level, but it was obvious that I will either queen one of my pawns, mate him, or win a piece.'

58.♘d5 ♗e4+ 59.♔d1 g3 60.♔e2 g2 61.♗f2 ♗e1+ 62.♔g1 ♗xh4 63.♗e2 ♗e1 64.b4

'If he just waits, one way of winning is to play ...♗b1 and ...♗xa2.'

64...h5

'It wasn't difficult to calculate that my pawns are faster.'

65.b5 h4 66.b6 h3 67.♗d3

'If 67.b7 ♗g3 and ...h2 mate.'

67...h2+ 0-1

'After 68.♔xh2 ♗f2 it will soon be mate.'

I thought the practical flow of the game came across beautifully in those comments, highlighting the moments where Keith was unsure and just needed to make a quick decision to save energy for later, as well as the reasons for some slower play (to avoid giving the white knight an outpost on d5 until as late as possible). Definitely recommended reading for some practical endgame inspiration! 3 stars!

■ ■ ■

And just to round off my review set I got attracted to the colourful cover of *A Modern Guide to Checkmating*

A Modern Guide to Checkmating Patterns
Vladimir Barsky
New In Chess, 2020
★★★☆☆

Patterns by Vladimir Barsky (New In Chess). The little twist to this collection of puzzles is that the chapters are organised not according to theme (like pin or fork) but according to the dominant piece (or pawn) that brought the mate to its conclusion. We have chapters both on individual pieces (like rook and queen) and on piece combinations like queen and knight. I won't say that this works perfectly – there were a few examples during a long combination where I doubted slightly why this example had been assigned to a certain piece. However, just like the Elk and Ruby series 'One pawn/knight/rook/bishop saves the day' the hint of which piece will deliver the final blow 'turbo charges' your solving efforts, making it a very pleasant solving experience.

The first chapter (on the rook) is one of the most attractive ones and I'll leave you with a charming example that made me smile when I solved it!

Krush-Stefanova
Krasnoturinsk 2004
position after 31...♖c7
White to play and win!

32.♕b8+ ♖c8 33.♕d6+

1-0, as 33...♗xd6 34.♖d7 is mate! Nice!

A nice solving experience! 3 stars! ■

They are The Champions

Many chess players have nostalgic feelings about Linares and the legendary 'super torneo' that was organized there from 1988 to 2010. It was great to see chess players returning to the holy ground of Hotel Anibal for the 2020 Spanish championship.

In-person events have an inherent risk these days. The championship was a 9-round Swiss with 139 participants. At the start, four players tested positive, and they were not allowed to play. Players who had been in close contact with the positively tested players were quarantined. In the end, 30 players dropped out.

The highest scoring woman was awarded the women's title. IM Sabrina Vega Gutierrez finished clear first with 6 out of 9 points, claiming her seventh title (2008, 2012, 2015, 2017, 2018, and 2019). In the nine rounds, she faced (and beat) only one female player, WCM Leyre Abrisqueta Zudaire.

In Round 8, Sabrina scored a critical win against Diego Vergara Anton with a nice attack:

SABRINA VEGA GUTIERREZ
Spain

Sabrina Vega Gutierrez (2380)
Diego Vergara Anton (2151)
Linares ch-ESP 2020

position after 20...0-0

Black is a pawn up. White is better developed and launches an attack, lever-aging the opposite-coloured bishops. **21.♖c3** The first part of the Rover: Rook Up and Over. **21...♗a6?!** Underestimating the strength of White's attack. **22.♖g3** Part 2 of the Rover. Now White is winning. **22...♔h8 23.♗g5! ♖ac8 24.♕h4 ♖c4** Black also loses after 24...♕c7 25.♗h6! ♖g8 26.♖xg7!! ♖xg7 27.♕f6 ♖cg8 28.♖c1. White gets a second Rover with h4/♖c3-g3 or ♖c6-d6-d8. **25.♗f6!** Ignoring the attack on the queen and threatening mate. **25...♖xh4 26.♗xg7+ ♔g8 27.♗f6+** 1-0.

Sabrina believes that chess makes you stronger in life. In 1999, she was competing for a medal in the girls' U-12 World Championship. She accepted a draw in the last round, convinced that this would earn her a medal. In the end, she finished fourth on tiebreak. When she lost on time in a winning position in the fifth round of the European Championship in 2016, she was undeterred. She continued to fight, beating Alek-sandra Goryachkina along the way, and finished shared first (silver on tiebreak), the biggest success in her chess career.

Sabrina Vega Gutierrez (2375)
Aleksandra Goryachkina (2485)
Mamaia ch-EUR 2016

position after 9...dxe4

10.c5 Black lacks space, and White threatens to consolidate with a3 and win the bishop pair. Black decides to grab the a2-pawn. **10...♕xa2 11.♗c4 ♕a5 12.♔e2** Now ♘xe4 is a threat. **12...h6 13.♖a1!** An important intermediate move to keep the initiative. **13...♕c7 14.♗f4 e5 15.♗g3 ♘xc5?** Black sacrifices a piece for two pawns and some initiative, but it is not enough. **16.dxc5 ♗g4+ 17.f3 exf3+ 18.gxf3 ♗f5 19.♕b3 ♗xc5 20.♖hc1 ♗b6 21.♕c3** and White won.

The coming months Sabrina plans to continue to work on her game, play a few simuls, teach her students online, record videos for chess24. And she is considering playing over the board again at the Sunway Sitges International Tournament in December. ∎

In **They are The Champions** we pay tribute to national champions across the globe. For suggestions please write to editors@newinchess.com.

Chess Pattern Recognition

ARTHUR VAN DE OUDEWEETERING

Doubled pawns must be pushed!

No need to wait passively for your opponent to take aim at your doubled pawns. Choose the proper moment to push and change the dynamics!

Vishy Anand
Boris Gelfand
Moscow WCh match 2012 (12)
Sicilian Defence, Rossolimo Variation

1.e4 c5 2.♘f3 ♘c6 3.♗b5 e6 4.♗xc6 bxc6 5.d3 ♘e7 6.b3 d6 7.e5 ♘g6 8.h4 ♘xe5 9.♘xe5 dxe5 10.♘d2

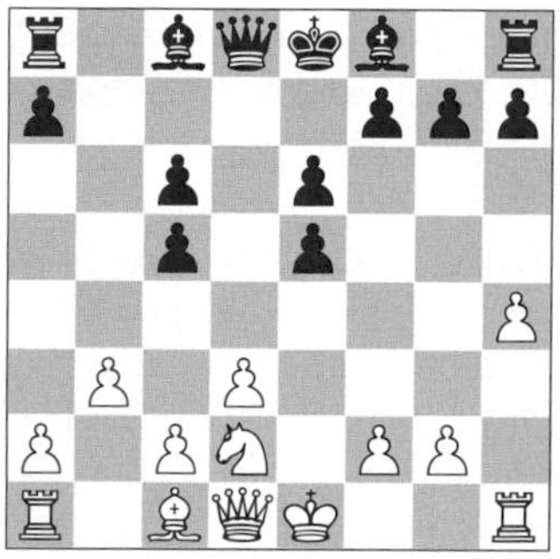

Gelfand had run right into Anand's preparation, involving a surprising pawn sacrifice. Due to the structural pawn weaknesses, Black is now in danger of ending up in a passive position without any prospects. Gelfand thought hard for more than 40 minutes and came up with a fantastic reply: **10...c4!!** Usually, if Black manages to get this break in, it is with the help of some tactic to get rid of the c5-pawn, which White intended to besiege. Gelfand immediately gives back his extra pawn, breathing life into his dark-squared bishop. **11.♘xc4 ♗a6 12.♕f3**

12...♕d5!? Again the most active. **13.♕xd5** 13.♕g3 would have exposed Black to more danger. **13...cxd5 14.♘xe5 f6 15.♘f3 e5** So now it is Black who has sacrificed a pawn, with a strong pawn centre and the bishop pair as compensation. **16.0-0 ♔f7 17.c4 ♗e7 18.♗e3 ♗b7 19.cxd5 ♗xd5 20.♖fc1 a5 21.♗c5 ♖hd8 22.♗xe7** Draw agreed. The weak d3-pawn and the possibility of ...a5-a4 do not leave White any hope of converting his extra pawn.

That surely was a difficult one to start with. The idea behind the advance of the doubled pawn in the following example, from a little-known game between two giants, is easier to grasp.

Mikhail Tal
Mikhail Botvinnik
Moscow 1966
Caro-Kann, Panov Variation

1.e4 c6 2.d4 d5 3.exd5 cxd5 4.c4 ♘f6 5.♘c3 g6 6.♕b3 ♗g7 7.cxd5 0-0 8.♘ge2 ♘a6 9.g3 ♕b6 10.♕xb6 axb6 11.♗g2 ♘b4 12.0-0 ♖d8

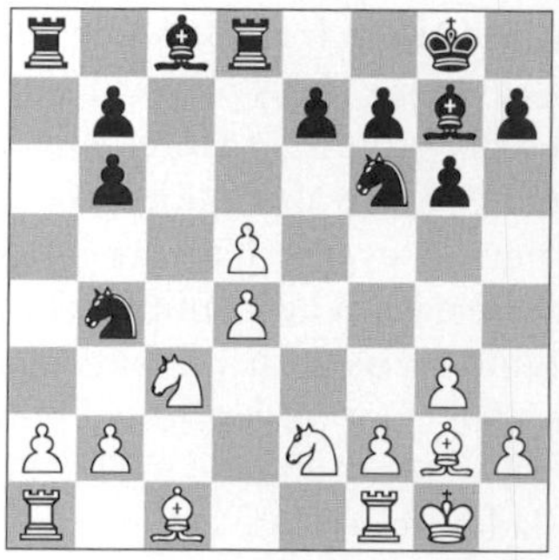

13.d6! White cannot hold on to his extra pawn in view of 13.♘f4 ♘c2, so he turns it into a desperado. **13...exd6** After this move, which obviously worsens Black's pawn structure, White's 13th has accomplished its goal. He is more active, has slightly more space and now also the better pawn structure. In his book *Zoom 001* Larsen even concluded that 'the rest of the game is a desperate fight'. That might be exaggerated, but 13...♖xd6 is certainly more logical for maintaining the pressure against White's isolated d-pawn. **14.♗g5 ♖e8?!** Black is struggling to complete his development, yet the active 14...♗g4 15.♗xb7 ♖ab8 16.♗g2 ♖e8 was the lesser evil, generating at least some counterplay. **15.a3 ♘c6 16.♖fe1 ♗g4**

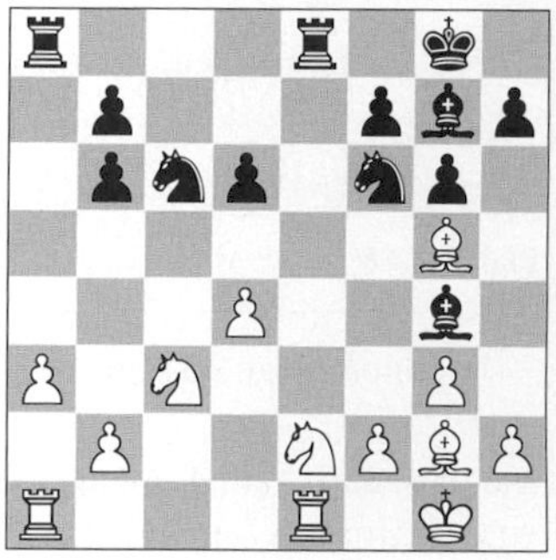

'Black has won a pawn, bravo! For the rest, his position looks pretty moth-eaten'

17.♗xf6!? Very direct and not dogmatic about the bishop pair. **17...♗xf6 18.♘d5 ♗d8 19.♘ec3 ♖xe1+ 20.♖xe1 ♖a5 21.♘e3 ♗d7 22.♘c4 ♖a8 23.d5 ♘d4 24.♘xd6** Now White is both a pawn up and more active. Botvinnik resigned on move 45.

Of course, being a pawn up makes it easier to throw in your doubled pawn, but even with equal material...

Yuri Balashov
Vitaly Tseshkovsky
Odessa 1968
Queen's Indian/Nimzo-Indian

1.d4 ♘f6 2.c4 e6 3.♘c3 ♗b4 4.♘f3 b6 5.♗g5 h6 6.♗h4 ♗b7 7.e3 ♗xc3+ 8.bxc3 ♕e7 9.♘d2 d6 10.f3 ♘bd7 11.e4 e5 12.♗e2 Initially, White played 12.♗d3, when after 12...♘f8 another pawn sac, 13.c5, led to the famous game Tal-Hecht, Varna 1962: 13...dxc5 14.dxe5 ♕xe5 15.♕a4+ c6? (15...♘6d7) 16.0-0 ♘g6 17.♘c4 ♕e6 18.e5 b5 19.exf6! bxa4 20.fxg7 ♖g8 21.♗f5! ♘xh4 22.♗xe6 ♗a6 23.♘d6+ ♔e7 24.♗c4 ♖xg7

when Hecht concluded: 'Black has won a pawn, bravo! For the rest, his position looks pretty moth-eaten'.
12...g5 13.♗f2 ♘h5 14.g3 ♘g7 15.♕c2 ♖f8 16.h4 0-0-0 17.d5 f5

18.hxg5 hxg5 19.0-0-0 f4 20.gxf4 gxf4

21.c5! Typical: activating the e2-bishop and vacating square c4 for the knight. **21...dxc5** 21...♘xc5 22.♗h4 ♕f7 23.♗xd8 ♖xd8 24.♖h7 ♕g6 25.♖dh1 leaves Black insufficient compensation. **22.♕a4 ♔b8 23.♗a6 ♘e8** Surprisingly enough, this natural move turns out to be a mistake. The counter-intuitive 23...♗xa6 24.♕xa6 ♘e8 was better. **24.♗xb7 ♔xb7 25.♕c6+ ♔b8 26.♕e6!**

Suddenly it becomes clear that Black is all tangled up. After:
26...♕f7 27.♘c4 ♖c8 28.♖h6 ♘g7 29.♖h7 And Balashov converted his winning advantage (1-0, 44).

It will not surprise you that these young masters might have picked up the idea from much older games, like this devastating attack.

Evgeny Kuzminykh
Alexander Budo
Leningrad 1939
Nimzo-Indian Defence, Sämisch Variation

1.d4 ♘f6 2.c4 e6 3.♘c3 ♗b4 4.a3 ♗xc3+ 5.bxc3 d6 6.f3 e5 7.e4

♘c6 8.♗e3 ♕e7 9.♗d3 b6 10.♘e2 ♗b7 11.0-0 0-0-0 12.♖e1 ♘a5 13.♘c1 ♕e6

Black does not fear the advance of the d-pawn. After all, this would grant him undisputed control of square c5, wouldn't it?

14.d5 ♕e7 15.c5! No, it wouldn't! **15...dxc5** Forced. **16.c4 ♗a8** Of course, White threatened 17.♗d2, but this move probably already made Black feel uncomfortable. Alas, 16...♗a6 does not work because of 17.♗d2 ♘xc4 (or 17...♘b7) 18.♕a4. **17.a4 ♘b7**

18.a5! Crashing through! The a-file has to be opened to proceed with the attack against Black's king. **18...♘xa5 19.♗d2 ♘b7 20.♖xa7 ♔b8 21.♕a4 ♘a5** White is completely winning now, and he quickly wrapped up the game. **22.♗xa5 ♕d7 23.♕a3 ♔xa7 24.♗xb6+ ♔xb6 25.♘b3** 1-0.

There is more life in your (extra) doubled pawn than you might think! Keep in mind these typical sacrifices and be ready to make a timely advance that will, for example, add new vigour to your minor pieces. ∎

Remembering Wolfgang Uhlmann

He was nicknamed 'the bookkeeper', but he was much more than only solid. The games **JAN TIMMAN** played against the best chess player East-Germany has ever produced, were full of fight and full of ideas.

Wolfgang Uhlmann, who died on August 24th, was born in 1935, the same year as Bent Larsen, whom I wrote about in the previous issue. Uhlmann developed slowly as a top player, possibly because he was taught to be a printer. As a citizen of the GDR, he also faced restrictions, as witness the notorious scandal when he wasn't allowed to play in the 1960 Zonal tournament in Berg en Dal, in the Netherlands.

Yet he travelled all over the world and became a successful tournament player. He did play in Buenos Aires in 1960, beating Bobby Fischer. On one occasion he managed to qualify for the Candidates matches. In the 1970 Interzonal tournament in Palma de Mallorca he finished in shared fifth place. He subsequently played well against Larsen in the quarter-final, but lost 5½-3½.

On *ChessBase News* Vlastimil Hort remembers that Uhlmann was nicknamed 'the bookkeeper', possibly as a reference to his education. It certainly suggests that he was first and foremost a solid player. My take on him was entirely different. I played against Uhlmann five times in the 1970s, and all those games were highly inter-

esting from start to finish. To me, he was a very inventive player. We played our first game in the 11th IBM tournament in Amsterdam. He had recently finished his match against Larsen, and at 36 years of age, he was at the apex of his form. It was my first grandmaster tournament on Dutch soil, and because we played each other in the first round, it was also a baptism of fire. It is no exaggeration to say that it was the most complicated game I had played up to then.

Wolfgang Uhlmann
Jan Timman
Amsterdam 1971
Grünfeld-Indian Defence

1.d4 ♘f6 2.c4 g6 3.♘c3 d5 4.♘f3 ♗g7 5.♕a4+ c6 Nowadays, 5...♗d7 is regarded as the best continuation. **6.cxd5 ♘xd5 7.e4 ♘b6**

8.♕d1 These days, 8.♕c2 is considered White's clearest way to an opening advantage. This move, incidentally, was already know from Flohr-Tolush, Moscow 1944. This is because it is highly dangerous for Black to capture on d4: White will get a mighty bishop pair and magnificent attacking chances. And after 8...♗g4 9.♘e5 ♗e6 10.♗e3 0-0 11.♖d1 White has a clear opening advantage.
8... ♗g4 9. ♗e3 0-0 10. ♗e2 ♘8d7 11.a4 a5

12.♕b3 Again, 12.♕c2 was probably White's best option. Black will not find it easy to create counterplay. If he goes for 12...e5, White will be better after 13.♘xe5 ♘xe5 14.dxe5 ♗xe2 15.♘xe2 ♗xe5 16.♖d1 ♕c7 17.f4 ♗g7 18.0-0. Black's problem here is that he cannot activate his knight.
12... ♗e6
Black changes tack. He abandons the ...e7-e5 plan and tries to create an initiative on the queenside.
13.♕c2 ♘c4 14. ♗f4 ♕b6 15.0-0
Now Uhlmann does sacrifice the d-pawn!

15...♘d6

It was less dangerous now to take the d-pawn, but after 15...♗xd4 16.♘xd4 ♕xd4 17.♖ad1 ♕f6 18.♕c1 White still has excellent compensation for it. This is why I decided to regroup: the bishop goes to b3, after which the knight can return to c4.

16.♗e3 ♗b3 17.♕c1 ♘c4

A good move in the fight for the initiative, but 17...♕b4 would have been more cautious. White doesn't have much better than 18.♗d2, after which Black can aim for move repetition with 18...♕b6.

18.♗h6

18.♗xc4 ♗xc4 19.♖e1 would probably have been slightly stronger. Black will lose his bishop pair when the white bishop appears on h6. White is slightly better.

18...e5!

The correct moment for this thematic advance.

19.d5 ♖ac8 20.♖e1 ♖fe8 21.h3 ♘f6

A vigorous battle is being waged with all the pieces still on the board. The position is equal, but both players must manoeuvre carefully to prevent falling behind.

Nineteen-year-old Jan Timman faces the highly experienced Wolfgang Uhlmann (35) at the 1971 IBM tournament in Amsterdam.

JOOST EVERS

22.dxc6

The correct moment to break the tension. Black is faced with a choice.

22...♖xc6 If Black had recaptured with the pawn, he would have wrested control of the vital square d5. The drawback, however, would

It is no exaggeration to say that my first game against Uhlmann was the most complicated game I had played up to then

be that the c-file wouldn't be opened. The computer has a slight preference for 22...♕xc6, intending to meet 23.♗g5 with 23...♕e6.

23.♗g5!

Changing the plan. White wants to exploit the availability of square d5.

23...♘d6 Another regrouping: Black has to protect square d5.

24.♕b1 White could have covered the e-pawn with 24.♘d2, at the same time chasing back the black bishop. After 24...♗e6 25.♗e3 ♕d8 26.♕c2 he would have a slight positional plus.

24...♕b4

More accurate was 24...♗c4, mainly to prevent the white bishop sortie to b5. The move's drawback is that

White could get a dominant knight on d5 with 25.♗xf6 ♗xf6 26.♗xc4 ♘xc4 27.♘d5. Black has compensation in the form of pressure on the queenside with 27...♛b3.

25.♗f1 Cautious play. I think virtuosi like Petrosian and Karpov would have gone for 25.♗b5. After 25...♘xb5 26.axb5 ♖cc8 27.♘d2 Black will find it hard to prevent White from exchanging on b3 and f6 and then playing his knight to d5.

25...♘d7 A sharp and ambitious move. The computer has a slight preference for 25...♖cc8 here, allowing Black to improve the coordination between his pieces.

26.♗d2 26.♗b5 was still possible, but it is less clear now, e.g. 26...♘xb5 27.axb5 ♖cc8 28.♘d2 ♗e6 29.♖a4 ♛f8! 30.♖xa5 f5, and Black has compensation for the pawn.

26...♘c4 27.♘d5 ♛c5

No pieces have been swapped yet, and the battle has not become any simpler. The text, for example, is a serious mistake: the queen is misplaced on c5. Black should have played 27...♛d6, keeping c5 vacant for his king's knight.

28.♗xc4 The first piece swap! Uhlmann is launching an offensive on the queenside. This looks like a good plan, but he had a stronger move: 28.♗g5!, although it must be said that this is a hard-to-find move. The bishop looks like having no business on g5, a square that seems more suited to the knight. But the deeper point emerges after 28...h6 29.♛d3!, and the black position collapses. So the only defence is 28...♛f8, vacating c5 for the knight after all. Even then, White will be better: 29.♖c1 h6

30.♖c3 ♘a3 31.♖xa3 ♗xd5 32.♗e3 ♗e6 33.♗b5 ♖xc3 34.♖xc3, with a strategically winning position.

28...♗xc4 29.b4 ♛d6 30.b5

Strategically speaking the strongest, but in view of all kinds of tactical considerations, 30.bxa5 would have been better. Play could continue as follows: 30...♘c5 31.♘b6 ♗d3 32.♛a2 ♛c7 (32...♖xe4 33.♖xe4 ♗xe4 34.♘g5) 33.♗b4 ♗xe4 34.♗xc5 ♗xf3 35.♗e3 ♗e4, and White is better, although Black also has some chances.

30...♖c5! The start of a positional exchange sacrifice giving Black maximum sway in the centre.

31.♗e3 ♗xd5!

The point of the previous move.

32.♖d1 Uhlmann increases the pressure. This is the correct practical decision, since we were both in slight time-trouble. But it would have been objec-

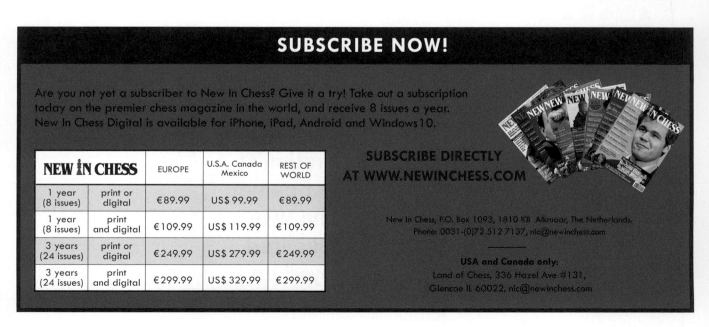

Donner was arguing how inventive a player Uhlmann was. The upcoming game made it abundantly clear

tively better to accept the exchange. After 32.♗xc5 ♘xc5 33.exd5 e4 34.♖a2 ♖e7 35.♘d2 ♕xd5 36.♗c2 ♗d4 Black has sufficient compensation for the exchange, but no more.

32...♘b6

The correct idea, but not the best way to execute it. 32...♘f6! would have given Black the advantage. Blocking the long diagonal may seem to be a drawback, but it is of no consequence. The knight is better placed on f6 than on b6. There are two variations:

ANALYSIS DIAGRAM

– 33.♗xc5 ♕xc5 34.exd5 e4 35.♘d4 e3 36.fxe3 ♖xe3 37.♕c1 ♖c3, and the white position collapses.

– 33.♘d2 ♖c3 34.exd5 e4 35.♖a2 ♕xd5 36.♘f1 ♖d3, and Black is better.

33.♕a2!?

An astonishing move that increases the tension. Remarkably enough, the database gives 33.♕b3, but it is impossible that Uhlmann, well-

known for his accurate calculations, played this, because it would have allowed an immediate black win with 33...♗xb3 34.♖xd6 ♘xa4.

A true alternative was 33.♘d2, since Black will find it difficult to move his bishop. After 33...♖c3 34.exd5 f5 the position is dynamically balanced. Accepting the exchange sacrifice would not be correct here. After 33.♗xc5 ♕xc5 34.exd5 e4 Black would reign supreme.

33...♖cc8

A mainly practical decision: withdrawing the rook brings clarity to the position. If I had had more time, I would probably have hit on the idea of maintaining the tension with 33...♖ec8. Strangely enough, it is also in White's interest to preserve the status quo with 34.♕a3, a possible continuation being 34...♕c7 35.♕xc5 ♕xc5 36.♗xc5 ♖xc5 37.exd5 e4 38.♘d4 ♖xd5 39.♘b3 ♗xa1 40.♖xa1 ♘c4 41.♖c1, and White maintains the balance.

34.♗xb6 ♕xb6 35.♕xd5 ♖c2 36.♖d2 ♖xd2 37.♕xd2 ♗f8 38.♕c2 A slightly hesitant move in time-trouble. 38.♖d1 ♗c5 39.g3 would have preserved a slight advantage for White.

38...♗c5 39.♖d1

39...♖c8? The last-but-one move in time-trouble and a terrible blunder. 39...♗d4 would have maintained the balance.

40.♘xe5 ♕e6

If White now withdraws his knight, the initiative will pass to Black. But he has another square for his knight.

41.♘d7! A rude awakening. The rook is cut off, making Black's position utterly hopeless. Black resigned. An abrupt end to a complicated game.

'Do you know Uhlmann?'

In the next IBM tournament I escaped from a lost endgame against Uhlmann. Three years passed before our third game – again in the IBM tournament, and again with me as Black. 'Do you know Uhlmann?' Donner asked me – he liked chatting just before the start of the round – arguing how inventive a player Uhlmann was. And if I hadn't already known this, the upcoming game made it abundantly clear.

Wolfgang Uhlmann
Jan Timman
Amsterdam 1975
Modern Defence, Averbakh Variation

1.c4 g6 2.♘c3 ♗g7 3.d4 d6 4.e4 ♘c6 5.d5 ♘d4

A dubious system that enjoyed some degree of popularity in the 1970s.

6.♗e3 c5 7.♘ge2 ♕b6 8.♘a4

The strongest approach; but 8.♕d2 is also good for White.

8...♕a5+ 9.♗d2 ♕a6

A curious move that was played very successfully in Keene-Bilek, Teesside 1972. That's about all the positive things you can say about it, except that 9...♕c7 also leads to a bad position after 10.♗c3.

10.♘xd4 Simple and good. Keene played 10.♘ec3, after which Black got excellent play with 10...♗d7.

10...♗xd4 11.♗e2

White usually develops his bishop to d3. 11.♘c3 is also fine. This would force Black to play 11...♗d7, since 11...♘f6 would end badly after 12.♘b5 0-0 13.♘c7 ♘xe4 14.♕c2 ♗xf2+ 15.♔d1, and wins.

11...♘f6 12.♘c3 0-0 13.♕c2

13...♗g4

The most principled continuation. Black wants to chase the white bishop to d3, and then withdraw his bishop and launch an attack on the kingside. Things remain precarious, though.

14.♗d3 ♗d7 15.0-0 A strong alternative was 15.♘e2. There could follow: 15...♗a4 16.♕c1 ♖fc8 17.♗c3

♗xc3+ 18.♘xc3 e5 19.0-0, and White is poised to advance his f-pawn. Black certainly won't find it easy to organize his defence.

15...♘g4

16.a4 The most ambitious move; but the cautious 16.♗e2 would also have yielded White a plus. **16...f5**

17.exf5

Uhlmann must have calculated pretty sharply here, because he is going for tumultuous complications.

The immediate knight sortie 17.♘b5 was objectively sharper, but this, too, required acute calculation. The main line goes as follows: 17...fxe4 18.♗xe4 ♖xf2 19.♖xf2 ♗xf2+ 20.♔h1 ♖f8 21.♗xg6!, and White takes over the attack.

17...♗xf5 18.♗xf5 ♖xf5 19.♘b5

19...♗xf2+ Black could also have captured with the rook, but this wouldn't have solved his problems. After 19...♖xf2 there could follow: 20.♖xf2 ♗xf2+ 21.♔h1 ♕b6 22.♕e4 ♘e5 23.a5 ♕d8 24.♖f1 a6 25.♘xd6 exd6 26.♖xf2 ♕e7, and Black may save his skin.

Amsterdam 1975. Jan Timman and his friend Hans Böhm go for a walk as Wolfgang Uhlmann is playing a sharp King's Indian against Genna Sosonko (0-1, 39).

ROB BOGAERTS

20.♖xf2 ♖xf2 21.♘c7

That was the idea: the queen has no squares.

21...♘e3

An attractive move, but it is not enough. I should have saved it for the next move.

The astonishing 21...♖af8!! would have forced a draw. The point of the queen sac is revealed after 22.♘xa6 ♘e3. White cannot cover f1 and g2 at the same time, making a draw by perpetual check inevitable: 23.♕d3 ♖xg2+ 24.♔h1 ♖ff2, and the rooks on the second rank will do their job.

22.♕e4! The best square for the queen, which is on its way to e6.

22...♕xc4

The point of Black's play. The poorly positioned queen has managed to join the fray after all. This is a minor psychological coup, but White has an important trump card up his sleeve.

23.♕e6+ ♖f7 24.♘xe3 ♖d8

25.h3! A controlled but strong little move. Black is relatively OK material-wise, but the dominant position of the white queen makes for an unpleasant position. The computer calls it winning for White, but over

the board these things are harder to judge. Still I do remember that I was seriously worried here.

25...♕d3 The only way to try and break the strangle-hold.

26.♗g5 He should have played his bishop one square further: after 26.♗h6 ♕f5 27.♖e1 Black will find it impossible to free himself.

26...♕f5

27.♗h4 Now the initiative swings back to Black. Better was 27.♖e1, since Black cannot capture the bishop: 27...♕xg5 28.♖f1 ♖df8 29.♖xf7 ♖xf7 30.♕c8+ ♖f8 31.♕xf8+ ♔xf8 32.♘e6+. An elegant combination.

27...g5!

Uhlmann must have underestimated this move. The bishop's elbow-room is restricted.

28.♗g3 ♖c8 29.♘b5 a6 30.♘c3 h5

The sharpest move. With 30...♕xe6 Black could have more or less forced a draw: after 31.dxe6 ♖f6 32.♖e1 ♖f5 33.♖d1 neither side can prevent move repetition without risking defeat.

31.♖e1

31.h4 was called for, with a dynamically balanced position. A possible

continuation is 31...gxh4 32.♗xh4 b5 33.axb5 axb5 34.♘xb5 ♖b8 35.♘c7 ♖xb2, with equal chances.

31...h4

The black initiative is assuming threatening proportions.

32.♕xf5

Otherwise he would have been forced to withdraw his bishop to the passive square h2. Yet this would probably have been better. The queen swap favours Black.

32...♖xf5 33.♗f2

33...♖cf8 The natural 33...♔f7 was stronger. After 34.a5 Black can play 34...♖b8, preparing the breaking move ...b7-b6. It looks as if Black has a winning advantage.

34.♗e3 b5 35.axb5 axb5 36.♘e4 ♖xd5 37.♘xg5 c4

Obvious, but 37...♖e5 was stronger: after 38.♘f3 ♖e4 the black h-pawn survives for the moment.

38.♘f3 b4 39.♗f2 e5 40.♗xh4

40...c3

The c-pawn will end up being pretty harmless. The alternative 40...b3 would have made it more difficult for White to defend. He will manage to generate just enough counterplay:

41.♖c1 (41.♗g5 is met by 41...e4!
42.♖xe4 c3!, and wins) 41...e4 42.♘g5
♖d2 43.♖xc4 ♖xb2 44.♔h2! ♖e2
45.♖b4 b2 46.♘e6!, and Black fails to
win by a hair's breadth.

**41.bxc3 bxc3 42.♖c1 ♖c8
43.♔f2**

White has defended well in time-
trouble, and is hardly worse now.

**43...♖c4 44.♔e2 ♖e4+ 45.♔f2
♖c4 46.♔e2 ♖e4+ 47.♔f2 ♖c5**

No draw!

48.♗e7 ♖c6

49.♗xd6

A sound decision. White sacrifices
his bishop to eliminate the advanced
black passed pawn.

**49...♖xd6 50.♖xc3 ♔g7 51.g4
♔f6 52.♖c8 ♔e7 53.g5 ♖d3**

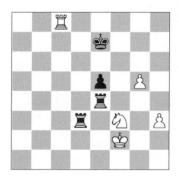

54.g6

A mistake caused by tiredness late
at night (we played from 1 to 6 in the
afternoon, followed by an evening
session from 8 to 10). White should
have left his g-pawn push for later.
After 54.♖c7+ ♔e6 55.♖c6+ Black
will be unable to make progress.

54...♔f6!

The winning move.

55.♖c6+ ♔g7 56.♘g5

It looks a bit threatening, but if Black
avoids all family checks, the white
pawn will eventually be captured.

56...♖d2+ 57.♔f3 ♖b4 58.♔e3

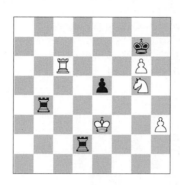

58...♖a2!

A well-known pattern: the black
rooks move away from the white king
in order to snare it more effectively.

**59.♔d3 ♖a3+ 60.♔c2 ♖g3
61.♘f7 ♖e4 62.♘d6 ♖f4 63.♔d2
♖xg6 64.♖c7+ ♔f6**

Here the game was adjourned for the
second time, and later resigned by
Uhlmann without being resumed.
I considered adding this game to
the selection of my 100 best games,
Timman's Triumphs, but the problem
was that White was winning in the
middlegame. In a looser selection, for
example of my 100 most interesting
games, it would certainly feature.

Tumbling into an abyss

So I escaped twice against Uhlmann.
But a year later, he was the lucky one.
In Skopje, I played White against
him for the first time, and managed
to break through his French defence.
But I failed to liquidate correctly,
allowing him to finish in second
place behind Karpov. Otherwise,
I would have been the runner-up.

We played our last game in Niksic,
again in the first round. It cannot
have been an easy game for him,
because on the way there he had
survived a potentially fatal accident.
Hort describes how a number of
participants were picked up by a
fleet of Mercedes from the airport of
Tivad. Hort and Uhlmann were in the
hindmost car. On a mountain road,

a lorry executed a dangerous over-
taking manoeuvre, forcing the driver
of their Mercedes to swerve and
tumble into an abyss. The Montene-
grin mountain roads were extremely
dangerous – they had no guardrails,
and in several places you saw impro-
vised wooden crosses with a number
plate on them. It was a lugubrious
sight – as if the crosses were meant to
commemorate the fallen cars instead
of their drivers.

The two grandmasters miraculously escaped injury. And Uhlmann
played an excellent game against me.
It was a high-quality encounter that
left the computer with very little to
find fault with. This is why I have
kept my comments to a minimum.

**Wolfgang Uhlmann
Jan Timman**
Niksic 1978
English Opening

1.c4 g6 2.e4 e5 3.g3

Uhlmann avoids the theoretical
discussion and aims for the Botvinnik
System in the English Opening. The
critical move is 3.d4.

**3...♗g7 4.♗g2 ♘c6 5.d3 d6
6.♘c3 ♘ge7 7.♘ge2 0-0 8.0-0
f5 9.♘d5 ♗e6 10.♗e3 ♕d7
11.♕d2 ♖f7**

A constructive move, first played by
Geller against Filip, Curaçao 1962.
Black is going to double his rooks.

12.♖ac1

Uhlmann opts for a move that I had
come up with. I played this rook
move twice in the 1970s.

12...♖af8 13.b4 ♘c8

The technical move that also features

Uhlmann played an excellent game that left the computer with very little to find fault with

with reversed colours in the Closed Sicilian.

It is interesting, by the way, that the thematic pawn sacrifice 13...f4 is possible here, the idea being to meet 14.gxf4 with 14...♘d4!, as in Nguyen-Predojevic, Budapest 2003. Black gets sufficient compensation for the pawn.
14.b5 ♘d8

15.d4
The computer shows a remarkable preference for 15.♘dc3 here. In that case, Black can make the thematic sacrifice with 15...f4 16.gxf4 ♗h3. And again, Black has that positional compensation because he gets a lot of clout in the centre.
15...c6 16.dxe5 dxe5 17.exf5 gxf5 18.f4

Strategically speaking the strongest move. White removes the option of advancing the f-pawn from the position, and only then takes his king's rook to the d-file.

18...e4 19.♖fd1
White has succeeded in keeping his knight in its central position. Another heavily strategic position with all pieces on the board has arisen.
19...♕e8!
Forcing White to show his hand.

20.b6!
An ingenious way to keep the knight on d5 regardless. White is threatening to take his knight to c7.
20...axb6
An attempt to keep as much play in the position as possible. 20...♖d7 would have yielded Black easy equality, e.g. 21.bxa7 ♘xa7 22.♗xa7 cxd5 23.cxd5 ♖xd5 24.♕e3, and there is little left to play for.
21.♘xb6 ♘xb6 22.♗xb6 ♖d7

23.♕a5
23.♕e1, to draw the sting from the black queen's sortie to h5, might have been slightly more accurate. After 23...♗f6 24.♘d4 ♖g7 25.♕a5 White

has some small measure of initiative.
23...♖xd1+ 24.♖xd1 ♕h5
The fight for the initiative is in full swing.
25.♖d2 ♗xc4

26.♘c3
After 26.♗c5 Black would sacrifice the exchange with 26...♘e6!. After 27.♗xf8 ♗xf8 White must play accurately to maintain the equilibrium. Only 28.♕e5 will do to preserve a dynamic balance.
26...♘f7 27.♘xe4
Now the play will get sharp.
27...♖e8 28.♗f2!
White withdraws his bishop in order to be able to transfer his knight to c5.

28...b6!
Black must continue to fight for the initiative as sharply as possible. After different moves he would fall behind.
29.♗xb6 ♗b5
Forcing White to play his knight, so that the e-file becomes available for the rook.
30.♘c3 ♖e1+ 31.♔f2 ♗xc3
Black gives up his bishop pair to force a draw.
32.♕xc3 ♖e2+ 33.♔g1 ♖e1+
Draw. ■

Willy Hendriks

CURRENT ELO: **2438**

DATE OF BIRTH: **21 February 1966**

PLACE OF BIRTH: **Boekel, the Netherlands**

PLACE OF RESIDENCE: **Eefde, the Netherlands**

What is your favourite city?
I've lived in or near Zutphen for the last ten years, a beautiful old city without the commotion of big city life.

What was the last great meal you had?
Well-deserved pancakes after a long forest walk together with my lovely wife.

What drink brings a smile to your face?
A Westmalle Tripel.

Which book would you give to a friend?
Vladimir Voinovich, *The Life and Extraordinary Adventures of Private Ivan Chonkin*.

What is your all-time favourite movie?
Johnny Cash's life story, *Walk the Line*.

And your favourite TV series?
Blackadder, from when I still had a TV.

What music do you listen to?
Music isn't as prominent in my life as 35 years ago, when I was buying new records at an alarming rate. The last CD I purchased a few years ago was *The Hits* of The Kinks.

Is there a painting that moves you?
I very much like the Impressionists, e.g. the painting that gave them their name, Monet's *Impression, soleil levant*.

What is your earliest chess memory?
I started playing chess some 41 years ago together with my best friend (back then and still now), we were completely hooked and played endlessly together.

Who's your all-time favourite player?
Gioacchino Greco. Though we know very little about him, the collection of games he left contains so much originality and good chess that I like to think of the rest of chess history as 'footnotes to Greco'.

Is there a chess book that had a profound influence on you?
Hans Kmoch: *Die Kunst der Bauernführung* (Pawn Power in Chess) and Alexander Kotov: *Think like a Grandmaster*. They are still good reads, although my own ideas about chess have drifted in a rather opposite direction.

What was your best result ever?
Trieste Masters 2007, my 2nd GM-result.

And the best game you played?
Modest silence ... Hendriks-Kollen, Dutch Open 2017, wasn't too bad.

What was the most exciting chess game you ever saw?
Rosanes-Anderssen, Breslau 1863 (0-1), is a strong candidate.

What is your favourite square?
The g7-bishop is my closest relative, it has been there all my life.

What are chess players particularly good at (except for chess)?
They form a community where everybody is welcome to play, also those who are, one might say, a bit eccentric.

Facebook, Instagram, Snapchat, or?
Since my team captain decided to communicate all team arrangements through Facebook, I had no choice.

How many friends do you have on Facebook?
By the latest count 410.

Who do you follow on Twitter?
No one.

When were you happiest?
When my first book *Move First, Think Later* won the ECF Best Book of the Year Award, I was extremely happy.

When was the last time you cried?
The day we had to let go our beloved cat.

Which three people would you like to invite for dinner?
Midas Dekkers, Richard Dawkins and Bert Keizer.

What is the best piece of advice you were ever given?
Stop playing that crap.

What would people be surprised to know about you?
I grew up in a pub. But people might have suspected something like that.

If you could change one thing in the chess world, what would it be?
Give us back our thinking time!

What does it mean to be a chess player?
You are very serious about playing; to compensate I take life light-heartedly.

Is a knowledge of chess useful in everyday life?
Hardly. If you want to learn something in life it's best to learn exactly that thing. Chess is best played for its own sake.

What is the best thing that was ever said about chess?
Someone once defined chess as 'solving too difficult problems in too little time', and I heartily agree.